PARAPSYCHOLOGY

AND

SELF-DECEPTION
IN SCIENCE

Books in the Same Series

by

R. A. McConnell

ENCOUNTERS WITH PARAPSYCHOLOGY
(1981)

AN INTRODUCTION TO PARAPSYCHOLOGY
IN THE CONTEXT OF SCIENCE
(Planned for 1982)

PARAPSYCHOLOGY

AND

SELF-DECEPTION
IN SCIENCE

EDITED AND
PUBLISHED
BY

R. A. McCONNELL

BIOLOGICAL SCIENCES DEPARTMENT
UNIVERSITY OF PITTSBURGH

The front cover shows Galaxy M81 as photographed through the 200-inch Mt. Palomar telescope by Milton Humason in 1952 and published in *The Hubble Atlas of Galaxies*. This galaxy, located in Ursa Major, is distant 9 million light-years. The light that made this photograph had traveled most of the way toward Earth before conscious man came into being.

International Standard Book Number: 0-9610232-2-8
Library of Congress Catalog Card Number: 81-90464
© 1983 by R. A. McConnell. All rights reserved.
Manufactured in the United States of America.
Printed on alkaline-buffered archival paper.
Book design by R. A. McConnell.

CONTENTS

1

ESCAPE FROM REALITY

R.A. McConnell

How important is scientific reality? How much are we willing to pay to know it ourselves and to have others know it? The present book will show that this is not an idle question.

By now enough research should have been done to allow scientists to decide about the reality of parapsychological phenomena—if we could but learn the essential facts of that research. Upon this point both skeptics and believers will agree. The problem is one of discovering the meaning of the evidence already in hand.

Each of us creates an imaginary world as protection against its real counterpart. We assemble a world view, piece by piece, over the years, until we have a comforting montage. In this process we ignore ideas that cause anxiety. We welcome the familiar and avoid the unknown. This description is as true in science as in the rest of life. Throughout our picture building we take care not to expose our innermost thoughts lest they be challenged. In this way we ensure our mental stability. These are not my insights but the teaching of psychology.

How much is progress worth? Perhaps it comes down to a question of values. Are we willing, like Lady Godiva, to ride naked before our colleagues so that mankind may escape the toll of ignorance? Or do we treasure our privacy above our sense of professional fulfillment? As scientists, are we engaged in a desperate search for reality, or are we members of a comfort-loving elite, paid by society to play puzzle games with nature? These are questions that might be asked of every scientist and that have a special relevance to parapsychology.

For more than thirty years I have pursued an understanding of parapsychology—not simply as a scientist, but as one who has striven unsuccessfully since adolescence to sample in depth all of human knowledge and experience. The perspective I have gained in parapsychology may be of interest whether or not it is acceptable. I found that what we now call parapsychological phenomena were described by another name in serious scientific papers one hundred years ago. It is a puzzling question why, four generations later, these phenomena are still ignored by scientists.

My investigations have shown that this question is not about parapsychology but about the whole of science. This book is offered as a contribution to the understanding of truth avoidance in science and also as a contribution to the experimental literature of parapsychology.

Skeptical scientists who suppose I am about to inveigh against their prejudice toward parapsychology may be surprised to learn that in the next two chapters I shall discuss self-deception among parapsychologists.

In Chapter 2, I present a paper by C. K. Jen of the Johns Hopkins University Applied Physics Laboratory. He graciously accepted my offer to publish his unexpected "parapsychological adventure" in the People's Republic of China after it was rejected for publication by the Parapsychology Foundation of New York. For the outsider who wants to understand parapsychology, his paper is important partly because of its substantive content, but even more because of the circumstances under which it was rejected by an American parapsychological organization.

In Chapter 3, I examine the fact that Chapters 4 and 5 are a pair of papers recently rejected for publication by the *Journal of Parapsychology* and by the *Journal of the American Society for Psychical Research*. The explanation of the rejections seems to be that these journals are pretending to be what they are not, namely, publications in an ordinary branch of psychology. In Chapter 3, I also pursue the results of this pretence, which I believe has led indirectly to the rejection of the field of parapsychology by the rest of science.

The first of the pair of rejected papers (Chapter 4) is largely a review of an experiment that I performed many years ago with the help of R. J. Snowdon and K. F. Powell. By providing new biographical and analytical information, this paper serves as an introduction to Chapter 5.

Chapter 5, a recent collaborative effort with T. K. Clark, describes some experimentally based insights about the nature of psychokinesis. We hope that these will prove fruitful to working parapsychologists and tantalyzing to determined skeptics. The layman who finds our statistical argument too difficult to follow in detail may nevertheless gain from it some feeling for the discovery process at a frontier of science.

In Chapters 2 and 3, I discuss self-deception by parapsychologists about themselves and about the world of science. This, however, must be judged in context, because I believe that self-deception is a characteristic of present-day scientists generally. To illuminate this idea, I obtained the reluctant permission of T. K. Clark to add as Chapter 6 a formal account of her experience as a graduate student preparing for research in parapsychology—an account that I had submitted earlier to a committee of the faculty of the University of Pittsburgh. Dr. Clark agreed only after she was persuaded that this biographical material might help scientists to better understand themselves and their students and perhaps might convince the layman that even expert scientific opinion should always be regarded with suspicion.

The opinions that scientists hold about scientific matters are determined by consensus and rarely represent an individual evaluation. This generalization applies not only to theories of great scope, but also to detailed experimental findings and specialized conceptualizations. Moreover, independent judgments made by competent scientists are generally of little value with regard to ideas on which no consensus has yet been reached. This is true because, like the rest of mankind, almost without exception, scientists are unable to think very well if their emotions are involved—as they always are to the degree that the subject matter seems important.

The foregoing paragraph provides one possible explanation for the failure of psychokinesis and extrasensory perception to be generally accepted as established phenomena of nature. Individually, most scientists who examine unfamiliar evidence are simply incapable of making a dispassionate judgment.

So bold an accusation requires documentation. Since there is no consensus among scientists with regard to the findings of parapsychology, unarguable evidence concerning the objectivity of scientists' thinking under emotional duress cannot readily be drawn from that field. Thus, it is a matter of regrettable good fortune that, in Chapter 6, I am able to present a case of emotionally induced group blindness concerning a scientific question peripheral to parapsychology on which an independent correcting judgment was subsequently rendered by the larger community of scientists.

Chapter 7 investigates self-deception in science at a new level of urgency. In January, 1982, I was invited to address my parapsychological colleagues upon a historical occasion of some distinction. I chose as my topic the future of parapsychology, and in the course of a month's intensive study I rearranged my thinking about the future of mankind.

The world faces serious problems. What I did not previously appreciate is that the solution of those problems must be undertaken in this century if they are to be solved at all. In Chapter 7, I describe how the runaway train of history is whistling down the track upon us. If we have not heard, it is because we prefer not to listen.

Our master problem is that we have lost our spiritual values. The solution may be to understand ourselves. If psychokinesis and extrasensory perception are real phenomena, they may be keys to self understanding.

2

SOME DEMONSTRATIONS ON EXTRAOCULAR IMAGE IN CHINA

C. K. JEN

EDITOR'S INTRODUCTION

The inclusion of the following paper by C. K. Jen in this volume has an explanation of some historical interest. The story begins in August, 1975, in the time of China's Cultural Revolution, when a remarkable document appeared in Scientia Sinica, *China's most important journal of science (Vol. 18, No. 4, pp. 573–580). Parapsychology was discussed under the title: "The rampancy of parapsychology and the decline of the superpowers." The following excerpts convey the flavor:*

> *Parapsychology . . . is a form of humbuggery that peddles the rotten products of superstition and religion. (p. 573)*

> *[The claims of parapsychology] are vicious attacks . . . unscrupulously launched on the theory of knowledge of dialectical materialism. (p. 575)*

> *In the struggle between the two lines of epistemological thought in the history of philosophy, parapsychology always belongs to the reactionary idealist camp. (p. 577)*

> *Besides using force and violence, the monopoly capitalist class also called upon parapsychology to play the role of priests in its suppression of the workers' revolutionary movement. (p. 578)*

> *Being according to Lenin "the most inexpressible foulness . . . and most shameful infection," parapsychology is used by the revisionists as a tool for deceiving the working people and especially for poisoning the younger generation. . . . The frantic craze for parapsychology in the USSR has aroused astonishment even in the U.S.A. (p. 579)*

> *Parapsychology is a pseudoscience which directly serves the interests of bourgeois and revisionist politics. (p. 580) .*

Scientia Sinica is China's English-language equivalent of the U.S.A.'s Proceedings of the National Academy of Sciences. *Challenged by the incongruity of this diatribe in an erudite journal of science, I sent parapsychological materials to the editors in 1976, and again in 1979, in unsuccessful attempts to initiate an international exchange of information in this field.*

Partially in consequence of the foregoing, I was considerably interested in March, 1981, when my departmental colleague, Lewis A. Jacobson, described to me a "parapsychological adventure" that had befallen his father-in-law, Dr. C. K. Jen, on a recent scientific (physics) lecture trip to the People's Republic of China. During his visit Dr. Jen had been asked repeatedly by his engineering hosts to witness children "imaging" concealed Chinese words—much as Americans, forty years earlier, had widely engaged in the "extrasensory perception" of card symbols.

I wrote to Dr. Jen, expressing a desire for a more detailed account of his experience and suggesting that this information might be generally appreciated within the field of parapsychology. Two weeks later in an hour-long telephone conversation, we explored each other's conception of science as a professional activity.

In May the herein-published paper arrived, and, with Dr. Jen's permission, I sent it to the Parapsychology Review, *which is parapsychology's leading newsletter. I also sent to the editor Dr. Jen's vita from* American Men and Women of Science *and an explanation of how I had acquired the paper and why I considered it authentic.*

The Parapsychology Review *is published by the Parapsychology Foundation of New York, which was established in 1951 by the psychic, Eileen Garrett, with money acquired by reason of her extrasensory powers. The* Review *prints on slick paper 176, 8.5-by-11 inch pages per year and in the past ten years has carried survey-type articles on subjects ranging over the Lama cults of Tibet (3[5]), African witchdoctors (5[4]), the teaching of parapsychology in American colleges (9[3]), and "hemispheric dominance and the existential shift." (9[5]).*

To my surprise, Dr. Jen's manuscript was rejected with the explanation that "it is not within the publishing program of the Parapsychology Review." *By a thirty-minute telephone call I learned in addition, (1) that neither Dr. Jen's use of the noncommittal term, "extraocular image" instead of "ESP" nor the fact that the P.R.C. is a faraway land had entered into the rejection, and (2) that "the policy of the* Review *is to construe parapsychology narrowly to include extrasensory perception, clairvoyance, telepathy, precognition, and psychokinesis," and that, accordingly, Dr. Jen's paper did not lie within parapsychology.*

When I asked why the guessing of concealed Chinese ideographs was any less parapsychological than the guessing of concealed American playing cards, the editor replied that she could say only that her advisers (whom she mentioned as including the President of the Foundation) had unanimously judged the paper not to fall within parapsychology. By way of added explanation, I was told that, for the same reason, the Review *had recently rejected a paper on "table tipping" in a seance.*

The foregoing circumstances make it desirable that I provide some additional background for Dr. Jen's paper.

Dr. C. K. Jen was born in the Chin-Yuan District of Shansi Province, China, in 1906. He had his college education in the United States, obtaining a B.S. in electrical engineering from M.I.T. in 1928, an M.S. in radio communication from the University of Pennsylvania in 1929, and a Ph.D. in physics at Harvard University in 1931. During 1931–32, he was a Fellow of the China Foundation, while also serving as Instructor of Physics at Harvard during 1931–33. He returned to China in 1933 and from 1934 to 1937 served as Professor of Physics and Electrical Engineering at the National Tsing Hua University at Peiping (now Beijing). During the war years, 1937–45, he served as the Director of Radio Research Institute of the National Tsing Hua University, and concurrently as Professor of Physics and Electrical Engineering at the National South-West Associated University at Kunming. He returned to the United States in 1946 as Research Lecturer in electronics at Harvard. In 1950, he joined the Applied Physics Laboratory of The Johns Hopkins University where he has remained ever since. For 16 years he was Supervisor of the Microwave Physics Group and Vice-Chairman of the Research Center. In 1967, he was appointed William S. Parsons Professor of Chemical Physics. At the end of 1974, he retired to being a Senior Physicist. In 1978, he became a Consultant to the Research Center of APL. His research has centered around microwave spectroscopy, microwave physics, quantum theory, quantum electronics, and radio engineering.

From 1972 to date, he has visited the People's Republic of China six times, varying from 1½ to 9 months each time. He is an Honorary Professor at Tsing Hua University in Beijing and also at the University of Science and Technology in Hefei, Anhui.

From a long list of his publications I have picked the following as representative: C. K. Jen, L. C. Aamodt, and A. H. Piksis, "Changes induced in the phosphorescent radiation of aromatic molecules by paramagnetic resonance in their metastable triplet states" (Pages 143–162 in The Triplet State, *Cambridge University Press, 1967). More recently, he contributed the section on "Zeeman and Stark Effects" in R. Lerner and G. L. Trigg (Eds.),* Encyclopedia of Physics. *Reading, Massachusetts: Addison-Wesley, 1980.*

I have known Dr. Lewis A. Jacobson and Dr. Linda Jen-Jacobson since they came to our University of Pittsburgh department in 1967. One of their areas of research interest is indicated by the title of a recent paper which they co-authored: "Control of protein synthesis in Escherichia coli: *Strain difference in control of translational initiation after energy source shift-down." (J.* Bacteriology, *1980, 142, 888–898.)*

At the request of the Dean of the Faculty of Arts and Sciences,

Lewis Jacobson has served since 1977 as a member of the University's "Interdisciplinary Committee for Psychological Physics," which has played a circumspectual role for the A. W. Mellon Educational and Charitable Trust in its financial support of my work. In this way Dr. Jacobson has gained some familiarity with the problems of parapsychology.

The Jacobsons have assured me that Dr. Jen's paper, which they had read before it came to me, is a sincere and competent account of Dr. Jen's experience—without regard to the question of the reality of extrasensory perception.

The importance of Dr. Jen's paper to parapsychology in my judgment is this:

1. It indicates that there is a stirring of interest in parapsychology among competent scientists in the P.R.C.

2. It displays an attitude toward parapsychological phenomena among adults and children in the P.R.C. that is strikingly different in flavor from what we find in the U.S.A. and Europe. We are privileged to listen to how they regard this topic when among friends.

3. The reported test results suggest that, under the right psychological conditions, ESP can function with a trial-success rate greater than 90%. This is contrary to the impression conveyed, as of 1981, in American elementary psychology textbooks (most of which now discuss parapsychology) but comes as no surprise to anyone familiar with the classic literature of the field.

4. Dr. Jen's paper illustrates how a Chinese-American physicist responded in courageous perplexity to unexpected evidence of psi phenomena. Such intellectual forthrightness evokes my personal admiration and may be inspiring to others.

Because the editor of the Parapsychology Review declined to explain the rejection of Dr. Jen's paper, I can only speculate as to the reasoning used. From a parapsychological point of view, the one unusual feature of the paper is the high rate of success in its ESP trials compared to what is seen today in most of the work from American laboratories. The staff of the Parapsychology Foundation may have felt that it would be unwise to report experimental results that some of their readers might find incredible.

It seems reasonable to suppose that the rejection of Dr. Jen's paper involves "self-deception in science." Some may argue that the self-deception was among the Chinese scientists who conducted these ESP experiments with children. Others may see the problem as with the staff of the Parapsychology Foundation in their assessment of the paper. The reader of this book may enjoy making his own judgment, pending the verdict of history.

—RAM

AUTHOR'S PREFACE

Accompanied by my wife, I undertook a lecture tour on recent developments in physics through three universities in the People's Republic of China from September 1980 through February 1981. Totally unrelated to my lectures or past experience, my attention was incidentally drawn to the upsurge of interest among the populace on some children's ability to have an extraocular image. This kind of interest was apparently stimulated by the first report in *Sichuan Daily* on March 11, 1979 about a twelve-year old boy being able to recognize a written word by his ear. In late 1980 and early 1981 when we were there, both the interest and activity in extraocular image had already grown to large proportions on a nationwide scale[1]. It was in this general atmosphere that our friends and former colleagues had urged us to be either spectators or referees for a few informal extraocular demonstrations. I will narrate our experiences on extraocular image; two in Hefei in central China and a third in Beijing.

THE FIRST DEMONSTRATION

This occurrence took place on November 24, 1980, in Hefei. After dinner, Yin Ke-neng (Lecturer in the Department of Radio Engineering), his wife, and son came to see us at our hotel with Zhu Jin-kang (a Lecturer in the same department), his wife, and their nine-year old son, Zhu Ji. Mr. Yin was one of the persons responsible for setting up my lectures at the University of Science and Technology of China. Mr. Zhu told me and Yin that only a short while earlier he felt that somehow his son had the faculty of Extraocular Image (henceforth abbreviated as EOI—my own notation). He thought that we might find it fun to give his son a try. My wife was willing to take him up on the offer and wrote with a ball-point pen, out of everybody's sight, the Chinese word meaning "sun" on a piece of paper which was folded into a small opaque pad enclosing the word. (See figure.) The boy traced the sample with his fingers and spoke out only part of the word at first and the complete word correctly at the end. My wife tried two other Chinese words in succession, meaning "level" (as in water level) and "sky." The boy was able to name the word correctly each time,

---

1. Zheng She. "Parapsychology, Is It Real?" *China Reconstructs,* Vol. 30, p. 50–51, January 1981.

Concealed Chinese words that were imaged by children in the presence of Dr. and Mrs. C. K. Jen on a visit to the People's Republic of China. *Top Three Words:* Imaged in a hotel room in Heifei, Anhui Province, *Middle Nine:* Imaged in a classroom at the University of Science and Technology at Heifei. *Bottom Three:* Imaged in the home of a Senior Scientist of the Institute of Electronics in Beijing.

although somewhat haltingly. When asked how he felt in tracing the word, he described that there was a tingling sensation in his fingers when they were right on the line.

Zhu Ji's performance surprised us very much because this was our first experience in seeing it done, even though Mr. Zhu apologized for his son's inexperience.

THE SECOND DEMONSTRATION

The second demonstration took place on November 30, 1980, in a classroom at the University of Science and Technology. Knowing about my interest in EOI from Zhu Ji's demonstration, Mr. Jia Zhi-bin (Proctor of the Hefei Associated University) organized a group demonstration and invited four children from the local Li-uan Elementary School. The children were Wang Wei-hua (girl, age 11, 5th grade), Liang Shu-jing (girl, age 10, 3rd grade), Xu Xiang (girl, age 9, 4th grade), and Duan Lian-yong (boy, age 9, 3rd grade). They were known to have some faculty of EOI to varying degrees. Mr. Jia had his aides prepare over one hundred samples, each consisting of a piece of paper, on which either a Chinese word or an English letter was written in color (red, blue, or black). Each sample paper was folded many times into a small pad, either sealed at the folding edge with a touch of glue or completely sealed. In any case, the writing inside each sample was not visible to the eye.

Mr. Jia opened the meeting with the four children sitting in chairs directly facing the front row and with an audience of some sixty University students and many students from an elementrary school associated with the University. Mr. Jia asked me to be the chief referee, with my wife and one other friend as assistant referees, all sitting in the front row directly facing the demonstrators. We saw an usher carrying a big plate of randomly placed samples to the demonstrators and let each of them take a sample at will. Each demonstrator put the picked sample between his or her palms. In less than a minute or two the three girls indicated that they already got their answers, Mr. Jia announced to them that each of them should write on the sample envelope the word and its color they "saw." These unopened samples were handed over to me and I then let them be opened one-by-one in front of us (three referees) and have the contents be compared between the inside and the outside. I then announced that Wang Wei-hua got the word meaning "male" correctly for both the Chinese character and its red color. Liang Shu-jing got correctly the red-colored word "Zhou" (best known as the Zhou or Chou Dynasty in Chinese history). Similarly, Xu Xiang got the word meaning "see" equally correctly. But Duan Lian-yong was not able to get any answer, and the poor boy sobbed for his failure.

As we were to go on with more demonstrations by the four subjects, on different samples, there arose in the audience an uproar among the elementary school students. We heard them calling out aloud why couldn't they join the the demonstration, even though many of them would be trying out for the first time. Mr. Jia and I agreed to let them have a try-out but limit the number of volunteers to five. Their names were Tang Qing-jiu (girl, 5th grade), Liu Shu-ling (girl, 5th grade), Liu Chun-yan (girl, age 10, 5th grade), Liu Jun (girl, age 5), Liu Zhong-jian (age 12, 5th grade).

The results of the second round of EOI demonstration are the following. Among the original invited demonstrators, Wang Wei-hua got the red-colored word meaning "broad" correctly (she had the sample crumbled in her hand), Liang Shu-jing got correctly a word, one of whose meanings is "public." Xu Xiang got correctly the black-colored word meaning "moon." These were their second round of successes. Among the new volunteers, Tang Qing-jiu first had the right answer for the letter "F" and afterwards also for the letter "G". Liu Shu-ling was right with the answer, the letter "M". Liu Chun-yan was the first and only one to use her ear in recognizing the Chinese word meaning "strength." Liu Zhong-jian was right about a Chinese blue-colored word, one equivalent of which is the preposition "for." Finally, the five-year-old girl, Liu Jun (younger sister of Liu Chun-yan) was right about the Chinese word meaning "up." One must say that the volunteers did as well as the veterans, because there was not a single failure among all the participants.

I was lucky to have Mr. Jia's permission for the referees to hold a short private session with the invited demonstrators. I asked the girls in what manner the extrasensory image came to them. The girls did not describe their impressions in exactly the same language, but they did agree on certain things which we'll temporarily regard as the common ground. Suppose the subject receives a sample between her palms; she needs a good concentration of mind. After a little while (a minute or so), she may feel a slight warmth in the hands or a certain tingling sensation. There seems to be something like a sensation on the move or a current going up from the hand(s) to the head (or the brain). An image begins to form in the "mind's eye." It appears first as a small colored blur and then gradually expands or enlarges into a larger and a much clearer colored image in focus. Finally, the subject "reads" out what she "sees."

THE THIRD DEMONSTRATION

The third demonstration occurred on February 6, 1981. On an impromptu visit of ours to the home of my former student, Yang Long-sheng, who is now a Senior Scientist at the Institute of Electronics, we bumped into a gathering of Yang's family of six (three generations) and two young sisters from the neighborhood. Yang suggested that, since the two sisters were known to be good subjects of EOI, it would be a nice occasion for us to witness at least the performance of the younger sister who recently won the first prize in a demonstration of EOI at the Institute of Physics. We were, of course, delighted with this opportunity and immediately welcomed the ten-year old student named Yu Po to proceed. We had, however, to pay the price of being the principal monitors of the performance.

In the first test, my wife went to a writing desk at the far end of the room, wrote something on a single sheet of paper which was then wrapped, and came back with a sample in a hollow wax ball roughly three-fourths of an inch in diameter (the ball consisting of two hollow hemispheres which could be closed, usually used as a container for medicine pills, available in Chinese households). Except for herself, nobody else knew what my wife actually put into the ball. The ball was placed into the hand of Yu Po, who quickly held the ball by both hands behind her back. In about one-half minute, Yu Po called out that she "saw" the red-colored Chinese word, one of whose many meanings is "Lord" in the religious sense. My wife quickly affirmed that the answer was correct.

In the second test, my wife repeated her secret mission and came back with a plastic box of roughly one-half by one-half by two inches. Yo Po put it in her hands behind her back and in about one-half minute announced correctly the blue-colored Chinese word, one of whose many meanings is "separate."

At this juncture, Dr. Lu Bao-wei, who is my former student and is now the Director of the Institute of Electronics, joined our company and was about to take us to his house for dinner. Seeing what was going on, Lu volunteered to make a sample known only to himself, and came back with his own wax ball. Yu Po handled

Lu's sample in the same manner and announced in the usual time that the word inside the ball was the red-colored Chinese word meaning "central," which was the correct answer. This amounted to a third test which was equally successful.

At the end of these tests, I requested the host to allow me to ask Yu Po a few questions. Yu Po acknowledged that her older sister (age 15) by the name Yu Yan could do pretty much the same thing. She then proceeded to describe her impressions about this kind of EOI with frequent nodding of agreement by Yu Yan.

Yu Po's description of her sensation contained details which were in some ways quite different from those of the Hefei subjects, but the principal conclusions appeared to be in gross agreement. She did not feel any warmth or tingling feeling in her hands when she received the sample. (It might be noted that Yu Po used thick containers enclosing the folded-paper samples in addition to samples in thin-paper wrappings, as in the Hefei case.) But, she first "saw" 12 different colored spots, only one of which brightened up while the others were vanishing. The colored bright spots appeared to be flashes swept from the right side of her head to the left (her sister, Yu Yan, nodded her assent), making flashes of dots or strokes somewhat disorderly. Finally, the whole image of the colored writing appeared clearly.

DISCUSSION

There are some major questions that can be asked of the type of EOI demonstration represented above. We will try to discuss them in the following order.

1) Is the EOI phenomenon *real* in nature? It would be a real phenomenon in a given act or demonstration if no fraud is involved in the whole process. To prove that the EOI phenomenon is indeed real, we insist that only *one* single *repeatable* "honest-to-goodness" case is needed for the establishment of the objective reality, even if many other EOI demonstrations can be proved to be fraudulent. That one single case, however, must be proved to be rigorously and completely free from any kind of fraud. This kind of proof is admittedly very hard to come by but must be achieved beyond any reasonable trace of doubt.

To illustrate the point, I would like to take up the case of the Third Demonstration where my wife did two EOI experiments with the subject Yu Po, involving a colored Chinese word written inside a paper pad which was itself contained in a wax ball and the other involving a similar situation with a plastic box. A fraud may have been committeed as a result of certain special acts among three persons: Yu Po, my wife, and a third person, X. Case (i): Yu Po may be a "psychic"[2] who could read my wife's mind or the sample directly, or she may be a magician who could play tricks with the sample. However, Yu Po is only a ten-year old student, not known by the Yang family, who are close neighbors, to be either a psychic or magician. The host, Yang, being my former student and having had a close relationship with me for many decades, would not knowingly subject me to seeing an act of deception without telling me the truth. Case (ii): An act of collusion between Yu Po and my wife was obviously out of the question. Case (iii): The person X could be a psychic, a magician, or an ordinary person. First, if X were a psychic, that person might be able to read my wife's mind and then transfer the information content to Yu Po by some act. But Yu Po showed not the slightest indication that she was being influenced by anybody, certainly not within one-half minute's time, when she gave the right answer. Secondly, if X were a magician, the person would need to play tricks with my wife's privately prepared sample and from a distant point transfer the real sample to Yu Po and/or play another trick to reveal the information to her. There was no evidence that these complicated magician's acts were performed, and the required time for it was rather too short. Thirdly, if X were an ordinary person, such a person was not at any time or place close enough to my wife (to the best of her knowledge) to spy on her information and then somehow signal the information to Yu Po. There was no indication that a person (or persons) performed such a delicate spy and delivery job for either one of the two experiments. Again, shortness of time (about one-half minute) would make the operation hardly practicable.

Having gone over all the imagined possibilities of fraud on a specific EOI demonstration we witnessed, we found none of the suspicions well founded. I am left with no better alternative than to assume the observed phenomena were indeed real.

In a broad sense, I have no reason at all to suppose any of the

---

2. A "psychic" is defined by Webster's *Third International Dictionary* as "a person apparently sensitive to nonphysical forces." In this paper, a psychic is introduced only for the sake of argument. We do not believe such a person really exists.

three demonstrations we eye-witnessed was in any way fraudulent. In the same vein, we heard that virtually hundreds of demonstrations or experiments on EOI involving young children have been conducted all over China during the past two years and, in general, the results were about the same as ours. If most, if not all, of these acts are fraudulent, then one would have to assume that multitudes of Chinese people are freely joined in a widespread act of conspiracy and deception. Such an assumption would be utterly unthinkable.

2) What is the explanation of the EOI phenomenon? Assuming that EOI is a real phenomenon, the first question is whether the phenomenon can be explained in terms of known physical forces. The answer has to be a negative one at the present stage of knowledge. Let us examine, however, what these known physical forces can do. There are only four known physical forces: the strong force of nuclear origin, the familiar electromagnetic force, the weak force of the elementary particle origin (or of the nuclear radioactive decay), and the gravitation force which is ubiquitously present between any two masses. The only force that can be applied to human bodies is the electromagnetic force. The other three forces apparently have no particular relevance. Human bodies are known to radiate and absorb radiations at microwave and infrared frequencies but they also absorb x-rays, gamma rays and even cosmic rays. Similarly, words written in color can emit and absorb radiation from very low frequencies through microwave and millimeter waves, infrared, and visible (perhaps even including ultraviolet to x-rays and beyond). But, such radiations are usually extremely weak and can be partially or wholly blocked by certain intervening materials. Hypothetically speaking (overlooking the extraordinarily small intensities at the moment) when such a radiation enters the human body at a crucial spot known to the Chinese as an "acupuncture point," and through the skin to the nerve endings at the location, electric impulses could be generated and travel through nerve fibers to the cerebrum of the brain. There the information content carried by the impulses could be processed by the human brain "computer" whose immense function, intellect, and maneuverability exceed, except for the speed, those of the present man-made computers by large orders of magnitude. The net result of EOI from the cerebrum "computer" would then be an output that can perhaps be displayed as a "mental image," somewhat similar to what appears on a television screen.

The above description based upon the presumed action of an electromagnetic force gives a very simplistic and totally inadequate mechanism, both qualitatively and quantitatively, of how an EOI phenomenon might work in a human body. This inadequacy may be in part due to our lack of understanding of the implied super high sensitivity toward EOI by children (particularly the girls) around the age of ten and some mysterious power of interaction, realizable in a human system, with an extraordinarily weak signal.

If we accept the EOI phenomenon as real and a rational explanation by way of known physical forces is wanting, the scientific world should explore a new frontier of knowledge in the biophysical domain, such as a modern interpretation of the Chinese traditional concept of Ch'i, translatable as "energy" or "vital energy," which in its rhythmic circulation around the human body may allow an enormous amount of power concentrated at a spot (say, an acupuncture point) for a short period of time.

EDITOR'S POSTSCRIPT

While this book was going to press, I happened to read a letter-to-the-editor of the Journal of the (London) Society for Psychical Research *(51, 181–183, October, 1981) which described an experience similar to that of Dr. Jen.*

In August, 1980, Dr. Lee C. Teng of the Fermi National Accelerator Laboratory at Batavia, Illinois, made a lecture stop at the Institute for Modern Physics at Lanchou, P.R.C. While there, he and his wife and son were invited by his hosts to participate in an ESP experiment with the 12-year-old son of an Institute librarian. As Dr. Teng described in his letter, the boy percipient, Su Peng, reproduced with pen and paper—and often quite quickly—what Dr. Teng had secretly written on a small sheet of soft paper which he wrinkled into a ball and inserted into the boy's ear. Su Peng successfully reproduced both Chinese characters and physics terminology in English, although he could speak no English.

Dr. Teng is listed in the 14th Edition of American Men and Women of Science *as a theoretical physicist with research interests in high energy and nuclear physics and in quantum field theory. He is Associate Director for Advanced Projects in the Accelerator Division of the Fermi National Accelerator Laboratory. I telephoned Dr. Teng at Batavia, and he graciously confirmed that he was the author of the letter described above.*

—RAM, 4 January 1982

3

THE ROLE OF THE JOURNAL
IN PARAPSYCHOLOGY

R. A. McConnell

The Search for Consensual Acceptance

Parapsychologists must share with orthodoxy the blame for the present neglect of their field. When said by a parapsychologist, this statement needs explanation.

Almost from the beginning of his career J. B. Rhine believed that, before it could be recognized as a science, parapsychology must have a professionally scientific journal—one that devoted itself exclusively to reports of experiments done in the tradition of Western science. In 1937, with the support of William McDougall, he created the *Journal of Parapsychology,* which in format, editing, and statistical sophistication ranks with the best of the journals of psychology.

The *Journal of Parapsychology* has published for 45 years and never missed an issue. It has pushed out an endless stream of papers, some strong, some weak, but all presented with a sober earnestness that should have caught the favorable attention of scientists from related areas. Whatever else, by now parapsychology should have been accepted at least as a legitimate specialized field of research. What, in fact, is its standing?

In fiscal 1981 the Federal Government of the United States spent $4.9 billion on basic scientific research but, so far as I have learned, nothing on parapsychology.

Among U.S.A. academic psychologists, approximately five percent consider ESP to be an established fact of nature, while 34 percent consider it to be an impossibility (Wagner & Monnet, 1979).

Science, the nation's leading journal serving all scientists, has consistently refused to publish experimental papers in parapsychology. Nevertheless, a professional statistician (Diaconis, 1978) was allowed six pages in *Science* on the pretext of presenting quantitative insights about a methodological problem in parapsychology (guessing the "closed" card deck), when in fact that problem had been explored mathematically 36 years earlier in a standard reference work of parapsychology (Pratt, Rhine, Smith, Stuart, & Greenwood, 1940). A major part of the Diaconis paper was devoted to nonmathematical criticism of informal experiments that all agree are of no evidential value. Subsequently, a parapsychologist, whose serious work was listed and disparaged but not discussed in this article, was denied access to *Science* for a reply (Kelly, 1979). Moreover, *Science* promised to publish a group of letters on the Diaconis article in a later issue (*202*, 1145, footnote) and then failed to do so.

Under the aegis of the intellectually liberal magazine, *Humanist,* a "Committee for the Scientific Investigation of Claims of the Paranormal" began several years ago derisively associating parapsychology with popular occultism (Rockwell, Rockwell, & Rockwell, 1978).

In a paper, orally presented and then released to the press at an annual meeting of the American Association for the Advancement of Science in Houston, Texas, on 8 January 1979, John A. Wheeler, an eminent nuclear physicist, publicly urged that the Parapsychological Association be disaffiliated from the AAAS. "Drive the pseudos out of the workshop of science" was the way he put it. "Nor is there in this proposal any intention to deny investigators full freedom of speech and a forum for their fribbles. There is forum enough already in a country that can afford 20,000 astrologers and only 2000 astronomers."[1] (Subsequently distributed on audio tape by the AAAS, reprinted in the 17 May 1979 *New York Review of Books,* and formally published in the AAAS Symposium Series [Wheeler, 1981]). Although he later publicly retracted certain libelous statements made about J. B. Rhine on this occasion (Wheeler, 1979), this physicist was clearly unrepentent.

---

1. For the lay reader it should perhaps be explained that what parapsychology and astrology have in common are the last five letters of their names. Wheeler has often been mentioned as a candidate for a Nobel Prize in physics. What shall we say when a mind capable of great precision publicly damns parapsychology by false association? It would be generous to call this a case of self-deception in science.

Collectively, the above miscellaneous items strongly suggest that there has been no consensual acceptance by the scientific community of the scientific legitimacy of parapsychology.

WHAT ORTHODOXY EXPECTS

What went wrong with J. B. Rhine's plan to obtain acceptance for his field by publishing the best available research in a conservative journal of conventional excellence?

The phrasing of the question suggests the answer. The *Journal of Parapsychology* follows the model of a journal of "normal science"—to use Thomas Kuhn's terminology. Parapsychology, on the other hand, is still in its "preparadigm" stage (McConnell, 1968). What, then, is it that orthodoxy wants of parapsychology? The answer: Much more than is necessary and customary in normal science.

When faced with a new phenomenon, orthodoxy wants, first of all, to be reassured as to the honesty and competence of the experimental Marco Polo. Pseudoscience is not a game that orthodoxy wants to play.

Our most competent parapsychologists, rightfully satisfied with the technical quality of their own research, have stubbornly ignored the disdain in which their field is held by nearly all outstanding experimental psychologists and physicists in our larger universities. Because our numbers are few, we parapsychologists have tolerated and even approved a great amount of sloppy research from our colleagues. Some of our better experimenters have further muddied the critical waters by associating professionally with nonscientists claiming to be parapsychologists. In short, we have fallen victims of the egalitarian malaise that has destroyed intellectual standards everywhere save in a few islands of excellence.

Trust in a fellow scientist comes from knowledge of him. Whereas in normal-science papers, any revelation of the personality and professional qualifications of the experimenter is considered superfluous and therefore in bad taste, in a preparadigm field the wise skeptic will discount almost entirely experimental reports from strangers. Hence, if parapsychologists are somehow to become more than a closed group of mutual admirers, we must display ourselves as individuals to outside scientists. One place to do this is within experimental reports. This requires a degree of flexibility and judgment that has simply been lacking in the management of our two American journals of parapsychology.

Assurance of honesty and competence is not enough, however. Orthodoxy must feel challenged before it will pay attention to a new discovery. Scientists love puzzles but fear change. An anomalous break in an old pattern threatens the collective peace of mind; while a new pattern beckons the scientific mind to play. Thus, scientists are decidedly ambivalent about any strange discovery, and it is part of the task of the explorer to allay the fears of his timid stay-at-home colleagues.

To do this, the explorer asks: Are there any structural clues in the new data that might be fitted into a pattern? (A mystery without clues is no challenge.) If there is a pattern, what is its meaning? Claims for a strange phenomenon should ideally be accompanied by explanatory speculation at a level appropriate to the data. (Large-scale theorizing, not closely tied to the data, is not acceptable.)

From the beginning of the scientific study of psi phenomena one hundred years ago, investigators found anomaly but little pattern. Mating the first pieces of the puzzle so that pattern might emerge has taken longer than anyone expected. Meanwhile, we have notably failed to gain the interpersonal confidence of the skeptics as to our competence and honesty.

EDITORIAL IMPASSE

In 1979 Dr. Thelma Clark and I completed some research that we believed held unusual scientific promise. We felt that, if this work could be properly presented, it might provide just what orthodoxy wants: an assurance of competence and the challenge of pattern. Our findings were embodied in a coordinated pair of mutually supporting papers. Here, we thought, was an opportunity to help achieve Rhine's original educational purpose by publishing these papers in the *Journal of Parapsychology*.

The editors of the *Journal* thought otherwise. Evidently those features of the papers that appealed to us were little appreciated. The nature of the problem can be studied in the following letter, which I sent to the editors of that journal and which is printed here in somewhat shortened form.

7 December 1979

Dear Editors:

Thank you for your letter of 26 November responding to the two papers offered to you on 11 September and 9 October 1979.

In summarizing his objections, your referee for the first paper said: "Everything considered, I find the paper to be overly defensive in a manner that is likely to be offensive both to parapsychologists and to scientists in other areas. I question whether the potential good to be hoped for through publication would offset the likely damage that could result."

Your referee is of the opinion that the paper will be simultaneously offensive to both parapsychologists and skeptics. That is quite an achievement for one paper, but is it proper for you as a journal of science to concern yourself with the feelings of protagonists in controversy? Should you not instead be asking: Is the information in this paper interesting, true, and relevant to the unsettled issues of parapsychology?

Overall, it is a very strange rejection you have sent me—one of the most curious I have encountered in 32 years in this field. Permit me to explain this by reviewing with you what your referee has said that led you to decide that the *Journal of Parapsychology* is "not the right place" for much of the material in this paper.

I justify my assumption that your decision was based largely on this referee's comments by the fact that no reasons for your rejection are given in the letter transmitting those comments. I note with interest that your offer to reconsider the two papers (if they are combined and shortened) is coupled with the sentence: "If you can see it our way, let me know and I will then collect more specific comments from our discussions here and send them to you."

Your referee offered three numbered criticisms. The second of these has merit, and I shall deal with it first. He said: "McConnell's wording in this paper makes it seem that *all* editors were hesitant about publishing [the first report of this research a quarter century ago], whereas the facts of the matter are that McConnell declined to have the paper appear in the parapsychological literature because he wanted it published in a periodical where it would be read by more scientists."

I relied upon the context in the present paper to convey that information, but I agree that it should be made explicit that the early paper was not rejected by parapsychologists. [Since done by adding footnote 4.]

The other two criticisms (1 and 3) of the referee seem to me devoid of merit. Please bear with me while I explain the basis of my opinion.

The referee said: "(1) The manner in which McConnell emphasizes the superlative degree of control imposed in this research implies that all other research occupies an inferior position. . . . It is inappropriate . . . that it should be presented in a manner that implies that it alone is above criticism."

But was it so presented? My position was given unambiguously, I thought, where I said in the paper: "The best of the dice work before 1948 met all of the customary procedural standards of psychological research. Taken as a whole, in conjunction with the discovery of pervasive, intra-session, scoring decline effects, it constituted, in my judgment, proof of the reality of laboratory psychokinesis. . . . It seemed to me that an experiment of the utmost rigor would be worthwhile if it would lead other physicists to enter the field so that our knowledge of the nature of the universe might advance as quickly as possible."

The referee's third numbered criticism concerned the following brief discussion at the end of my paper, which he feared would offend skeptics: "The adverse reaction to our findings by eminent physicists . . . and the irrational reasons given by editors for rejecting our report . . . led me to conclude that the scientific leaders of our time would not competently examine empirical evidence for phenomena that do not fit their preconceptions of what is possible."

This was my evaluation of the situation a quarter century ago. My experience since then has confirmed its continuing truth. I have no doubt that the referee and all knowledgeable parapsychologists fully accept my evaluation.[2]

Where the disagreement lies is on the question of whether it is wiser not to speak this truth in public. I believe that most parapsychologists do not subscribe to the idea that skepticism will eventually be overcome if we are content as an in-group to enjoy our martyrdom in silence. Where do the editors stand?

The referee's third criticism included two patent reading errors. My quotation from the rejected paper as given above is essentially complete and makes no mention of "theory." [See the manuscript in Chapter 4 of this book.] Yet the referee mysteriously imagined that it said I have decided that orthodox scientists "will not give reasonable attention to the evidence for the reality of psi until they have been offered an adequate theory relating it to current scientific concepts." His gratuitously added comment that he "did not see that this paper offers anything clearly designated as contributing to such a theory" confirms his confusion.[3]

The referee continued: "Then McConnell goes on to say that he has personally advanced a long way toward acquiring an adequate understanding of psi, but he gives us no hint of what this is." This is a very remarkable statement, whose accuracy I would expect to have been doubted by anyone who knows me. Upon turning to the paper, you will see that my referent for the "understanding I now feel I have gathered in good measure" was clearly the contiguously preceding "belief processes of scientists."

[2. When carefully read, the conclusion is seen to be a very modest accusation, with which most orthodox scientists would also agree.]

[3. It is obliquely relevant that this referee had not seen our second paper, which appears as Chapter 5 in this book and which, indeed, has theoretical content.]

Because all of these incongruities from the referee were passed on to me without disclaimers or additional explanation, I am at a loss to understand the editors' thinking processes. In any case, the rejection of the paper must be evaluated in terms of its stated purpose [which you did not discuss]. In the paper I said: "recently, [Mr. Kenneth Powell] suggested that I prepare a review of our dice experiment because of the unusual precautions we had taken to ensure the credibility of our data and because of the continuing willingness today of many scientists to write off psi phenomena as a manifestation of nothing more than incompetence or dishonesty." . . .

It will not be necessary to discuss the criticisms [by another referee] of the second paper of the pair since your rejection of the first forces us to make other publication arrangements.

Sincerely yours,

R. A. McConnell

This was followed by a second and final letter, here reproduced in full:

7 January 1980

Dear Editors:

Thank you for your gracious letter of 14 December, amplifying and confirming the editors' decision of 26 November not to publish our two papers unless they were shortened and combined.

In my letter of 7 December I did not mean to imply that the editors accepted the referee's judgment uncritically, but merely that they agreed with it. Otherwise, they would have offered some other basis for their decision.

I appreciate your kindness in having a third consultant reduce to writing his thoughts about our first paper so that they could be sent with your 14 December letter. I note that these comments are devoted partly to matters of style and partly to matters of logic.

I shall not burden you with discussion except to say that in preparing the paper I considered all of these questions of logic and that my judgment concerning them differs from the consultant's. The consultant's comments on style amount to a reiteration of the editors' succinctly expressed opinion of 26 November: "The *Journal of Parapsychology* in not the right place."

I note the editors' renewed offer to send further critical comments from the staff of the Parapsychology Institute if we will agree to write a paper conforming to their model. I understand what kind of paper the staff of the Institute would like to see. I have written many such papers in my lifetime.

Again, let me express my appreciation for your efforts to discover ground for an author-journal rapprochement. Perhaps on some fu-

ture occasion we shall find our publishing objectives to be mutually
compatible.

Sincerely yours,

R. A. McConnell

A Second Judgment

Hoping to avoid the expense of private publication, we next
submitted our papers to the *Journal of the American Society for
Psychical Research,* which is a catholic serial intended for the
mixed membership of that Society. The editor's rejection is illumi-
nated by the following letter (given here in re-arranged and slightly
shortened form):

12 March 1980

Dear Editor:

I shall not appeal your 16 February rejection of our two papers. As
you know, the last four papers I sent you were rejected. This is an
interesting circumstance, suggesting that it might be worthwhile to
consider how these papers differ and what they have in common that
caused their rejection.

The first was a book review, for which you had thanked me in
advance. In it, to your displeasure, I criticized "left-wing expedi-
ency," i.e., pandering to the credulity of the public—a vice that is
costing parapsychology the support of the scientific community.

The second was an essay on adolescent psychology, a topic I believe to be immediately relevant to the public acceptance of parapsychology and ultimately important for understanding poltergeist
phenomena.

The third rejection was based on your referee's opinion that the
interest of the historical material in the paper did not justify publication in your journal. He evidently failed to recognize that this material is essential to establish the credibility of the experimental data
and to assist in their interpretation. Its historical value is incidental.
[This rejected paper appears as Chapter 4 in this book.]

The fourth rejected paper, which I co-authored with Dr. Clark,
was a theoretical contribution based on a statistical analysis of experimental data. [It appears as Chapter 5 in the present book.] With
regard to the "organizing principle," which this referee correctly
recognized as the central idea of the paper, he said: "In view of the
uncertainties of the evidence for it, I wonder whether more of a
verbal presentation and less of a quantitative presentation would get
the message across to more people and not leave out what is most
essential—which is, I think, the innovative theory rather than the
quantitative analysis." This strikes me as expressing a religious rather
than a scientific point of view.

These four rejected papers were about as diverse as any four papers could be. What they had in common was that they all reflected the philosophy of the principal author.

It is proper to review all scientific papers for technical oversights, but, when a paper comes from an author with a long record of sound, creative activity, science journals in well-established fields do not ordinarily allow referees to pass judgment on concepts, opinions, and intellectual style. That is what subscribing readers are for.

Sincerely yours,

R. A. McConnell

Samizdat

Because the *Journal of Parapsychology* and the *Journal of the American Society for Psychical Research* are world-foremost journals of scientific parapsychology, the rejection of our papers for what seem to us defective reasons suggests to us a weakness in the professional structure of the field. We believe the matter should be publicly examined. We also believe that our scientific work merits judgment by our peers. For these reasons we present our papers in the next two chapters of this book in the form in which they were rejected by these journals.

The first paper is offered for its evidential, biographical, and historical value. It may hold some tutorial interest as well. The section titled, "The Meaning of Probability in Multiple Analysis," is intended to clarify concepts concerning which there has long been confusion, both in and outside the field of parapsychology.

To encourage the reader to persevere in the second paper with what may seem a formidable task, I shall take him into our confidence at this point and reveal our tentative evaluation of that paper. We think we are on the trail of two, time-dependent, psychological factors that jointly determine the magnitude and sign of the running average of success in throwing dice. If so, this is the first occurrence in parapsychology of the kind of complex patterning that in physics, for example, has classically been used as the basis for theory building. Beyond that, we see a possibility that by the systematic exploration and manipulation of these factors we may be able to enhance and ultimately to control psychokinesis. This is a mere gleam-in-the-eye of a kind that in "normal science" one would pursue secretly while telling no more than was necessary to establish one's claim to priority. But parapsychology is not yet normal science, and we would like to hasten its advancement with all the help we can get.

REFERENCES

Diaconis, P. (1978). Statistical problems in ESP research. *Science, 201,* 131–136.

Kelly, E. F. (1979). Reply to Persi Diaconis. *Zetetic Scholar,* No. 5, 20–28.

McConnell, R. A. (1968). The structure of scientific revolutions: An epitome. *Journal of the American Society for Psychical Research, 62,* 321–327.

Pratt, J. G., Rhine, J. B., Smith, B. M., Stuart, C. E., & Greenwood, J. A. (1940). *Extrasensory Perception After Sixty Years.* New York: Henry Holt. (Currently available from Brandon Press.)

Rockwell, T., Rockwell, R., & Rockwell, W. T. (1978). Irrational rationalists: A critique of *The Humanist*'s crusade against parapsychology. *Journal of the American Society for Psychical Research, 72,* 23–34.

Wagner, M. W., & Monnet, M. (1979). Attitudes of college professors toward extrasensory perception. *Zetetic Scholar,* No. 5, 7–16.

Wheeler, John A. (1979). Parapsychology—A correction (letter to the editor). *Science, 205,* 144.

Wheeler, John A. (1981). Drive the pseudos out of the workshop of science. Pages 99–100 in R. G. Jahn (Ed.), *The Role of Consciousness in the Physical World.* Published by Westview Press for the American Association for the Advancement of Science.

4

WISHING WITH DICE REVISITED

R. A. McConnell

ABSTRACT

This is a historical review and re-analysis of a 1948–1950 experiment in which 386 subjects each threw 432 dice while wishing for faces corresponding to a pre-chosen target number. The final two-thirds of the dice for each subject were automatically photographed within a motor-driven, totally enclosing die cage operated by the experimenter. Although the total score of the experiment was not significantly different from chance expectation, a 3.8% decline in mean scoring rate occurred within the repeated sequence of 36 uninterrupted throws ($p = .005$). The author examines the chronological accumulation of this anticipated decline and of an unusually small first-order interaction, which was unexpectedly found. This experiment is of exceptional interest because of the precautions taken to meet all of the known counter-explanations of psychokinesis.

BIOGRAPHICAL BACKGROUND

In 1948 I undertook my first serious experiment in parapsychology, using a motor-driven dice machine newly built by Wallace B. Scherer[1] and generously lent to me by J. B. Rhine for use at the Physics Department of the University of Pittsburgh.

In this venture I had the assistance of Kenneth F. Powell (b. 1923), a graduate student in astronomy, and Ruthanna Johnson Snowdon (b. 1896), the wife of a Pittsburgh industrialist, who was to serve as my five-day-a-week unpaid research associate until 1961. Both are still members of the Parapsychological Association although not actively engaged in research. In view of the elusive nature of psi phenomena, I believe it might add to the value of our experiment if something were known of their backgrounds.

After raising her children and before joining forces with me, Ruth Snowdon had given a decade of volunteer service to Pittsburgh welfare organizations. Later, beginning in 1956, while she was gradually terminating her association with me, she held a working appointment for six years as Research Associate in Arche-

---

1. Subsequently, founder and executive officer of Psychological Instruments Co. of Richmond, Va.

ology at the Carnegie Museum of Pittsburgh. In her last 14 years in Pittsburgh she built for our Carnegie Library, by personal solicitation and public advertising, America's finest circulating collection of (80,000) colored travel slides. She was a skilled photographer and began the project by donating her own several thousand Kodachrome pictures gathered on trips with her husband to distant lands. (Her "Peru" series of trials in my paper, "Remote Night Tests for PK" [McConnell, 1955], was done in ten nights near Cuzco, after days exploring Inca ruins at 7,000 feet.) When she left Pittsburgh, her discriminating collection of 400 volumes on Central and South American anthropology was given to Chatham College.

Ruth had been a red-headed tomboy and the only daughter in a Philadelphia Main Line family. Her father, Alba Boardman Johnson, was the first president of Baldwin Locomotive Corporation and an eminent citizen of Philadelphia. Her mother was Elizabeth Thomas Reeves, daughter of the Biddle Reeves of Philadelphia.

Ruth completed her formal education at Vassar College in 1918 and came to Pittsburgh in 1920. By the end of World War II she was known and respected by the leaders of the city for her generosity, managerial competence, intellectual vigor, and gracious entertaining. It was surely the fact that she introduced me to Adolph W. Schmidt, President of the A. W. Mellon Educational and Charitable Trust and later ambassador to Canada, that led to my support by that foundation beginning in 1953 and continuing ever since.

Recently, to be certain that my own investigation was accurate, I asked Ruth Snowdon to prepare a summary of her service activities in Pittsburgh. Her final paragraph explains her interest in parapsychology:

> My twelve years' association with the University of Pittsburgh's parapsychology research under the leadership of Dr. Robert A. McConnell was the answer to my strong desire to accomplish something fundamental to understanding the needs of mankind. I felt that this study was an effort in the right direction. If it proved itself, fine—if not, it was a soundly conducted and worthwhile attempt.

Kenneth Powell was an ordnance officer in the Pacific Theatre in World War II. He is now a Corporate Marketing Consultant with IBM. Recently, he suggested that I prepare a review of our dice experiment because of the unusual precautions we had taken to ensure the credibility of our data and because of the continuing willingness today of many scientists to write off psi phenomena as a manifestation of nothing more than incompetence or dishonesty.

The need for the present pair of papers goes beyond history and credibility, however. The report that we published (McConnell, Snowdon, & Powell, 1955a) was accurate and complete at the time of its writing, but certain later analyses of the data deserve publication. Cautioned by the racing years, I am taking time to review my file on this experiment and to rescue from oblivion some findings that may be of importance.

In the present paper I shall summarize the experiment and give it an analysis of variance. In a paper to follow (McConnell & Clark, 1982) there is a study of what we have called "progressive organization" within the psychokinetic testing session—an effect that I believe has not previously been noted in the literature but which is so clearly shown in these data that I am inclined to accept it as real.

THE EXPERIMENT

In this experiment, 386 previously untested, mostly student volunteers each separately attempted to influence 432 die faces, thrown two at a time, thus yielding a grand total of 166,752 die faces. Each subject threw his or her first data page of die faces from a rough-lined cup into a tray, followed by two pages of throws within a motor-driven die cage. The testing time per subject was about 40 minutes.

The subject was instructed to wish to obtain as many target faces as possible. Each subject was allowed only one target number in the range 1 to 6. (Seven additional subjects who requested a change of target during the test session are omitted from the present analysis.) Thus, the nominal binomial probability of success was 1/6 for each die-face trial.

The die cage, 13 cm square and 90 cm long, turned about an axis passing through its center and perpendicular to its own long axis at a rate of one half turn every eight seconds. See Figure 1. The long walls of the cage were of transparent plastic, lined with rubber bumpers to randomize the fall of the dice pair from end to end. The cage ends were of padded wood. A solenoid-operated, single-frame, 16mm motion-picture camera received an image of the fal-

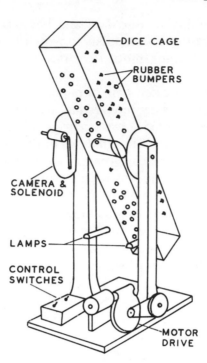

Figure 1. The motor-driven die-throwing machine, sketched from a photograph. Drawn in a turning position. The nonresettable counter for serially numbering each half turn is not visible.

len dice through a fixed periscope inserted along the axis of cage rotation. A picture was automatically taken after each half turn of the cage. In addition, the experimenter who operated the machine, recorded in pencil the number of spots (1 to 6) showing on the top surfaces of the (cup and) machine dice after they fell.

As indicated in Figure 2, the data pages were divided into six blocks or columns, three in the upper half page and three in the lower. The columns had 12 lines, each with space for entering two die faces and the serial number of the fall as needed. The unchanging target number was posted above each column as the test session proceeded. There was space below each column for recording the count of the number of target die faces (hits or successes) occurring in that column.

Three columns of die faces (36 throws) were always recorded without pause. At the end of each half page the data taking was interrupted by turning off the camera and its lights for conversation and for totalling of the target hits in each of the columns. The

PAGE 1   PAGE 2   PAGE 3

CUP-THROWN   MACHINE-THROWN

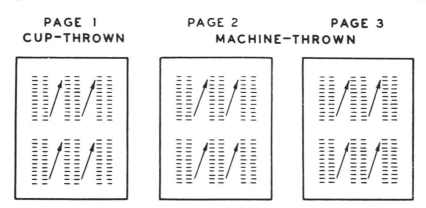

Figure 2. The layout of the three data pages used for each of the 386 test subjects. Each of the six double columns on a page had space for 24 die faces thrown two at a time. A rest period after every half page (72 die faces) controlled the emergence of psychokinesis.

cage continued turning, with camera and lights off, after each upper half page and was stopped completely at the bottom of each page.

The resulting total number of target hits in each of the 18 column positions of the three data pages is shown in Table 1. There was no significant total deviation from chance expectation for the experiment as a whole. However, as anticipated from previous die-throwing experiments reported in the literature, a statistically significant decline in scoring rate was found within the half page of the data. The average scoring rate was above chance expectation in the left-hand column of the half page and below expectation in the right-hand column, with the middle column near the chance level. This result is formally evaluated in an analysis of variance given below.

PURPOSE AND PROCEDURAL CONTROLS

Experimental work on the psychokinetic control of gaming dice began in 1934 at J. B. Rhine's laboratory at Duke University and was first published in 1943. It was *Time* magazine's mention of that work (July 26, 1943, p. 44) that first focused my attention upon parapsychology and eventually led to my beginning the present experiment in 1948.

The best of the dice work before 1948 met all of the customary procedural standards of psychological research. Taken as a whole,

Table 1

SUCCESSES (TARGET DIE FACES) OCCURRING IN EACH COLUMN POSITION OF THE
THREE DATA PAGES (EXPERIMENTERS COMBINED).

Number of subjects = 386. Number of die-face trials per subject for each
position = 24. Nominal p-value = 1/6.

Half Page	Page 1 (Cup-thrown)			Page 2 (Machine-thrown)			Page 3 (Machine-thrown)		
Upper	1572	1509	1544	1553	1585	1524	1636	1566	1518
Lower	1512	1520	1512	1572	1475	1509	1592	1566	1477

in conjunction with the discovery of pervasive, intra-session, scoring decline effects, it constituted, in my judgment, proof of the reality of laboratory psychokinesis.

The idea that the wishing of a bystander might affect the configuration of a presumably isolated physical system was, of course, appalling to me as a physicist. But at that time I was steeped in the operationalism of P. W. Bridgman and could do no less than say: "I must ignore expectations. What are the observable facts?" It seemed to me that an experiment of the utmost rigor would be worthwhile if it would lead other physicists to enter the field so that our knowledge of the nature of the universe might advance as quickly as possible.

It was in this spirit that I conceived and executed this experiment. The arrangements bearing upon control against self-deception have already been published (McConnell, Snowdon, & Powell, 1955a; 1955b), and I shall do no more than list them at this point:

1. Use of a fixed data-gathering pattern (one page of cup-thrown dice followed by two machine-thrown pages).

2. Use of each subject only once, in the presence of one experimenter and no observers.

3. The use of only one target number per subject, copied 18 times onto the data pages in the test session.

4. The use of an approximately random sequence of target-face numbers throughout the experiment, subject to the limitation that the numbers were not used equally often.

5. The use throughout the experiment of one pair of dice for cup throwing and a second pair for the machine, and the x-raying of all four dice to be sure of their internal structure.

6. Control for dice bias by scoring all die faces successively for all six possible target numbers and then comparing the target with the nontarget scores for each target number.

7. The turning of the transparent, totally enclosing, plastic die cage at 7.5 half-turns per minute by a constant-speed motor with a 3.1-second reading pause in the upright position—the entire motion being controlled by a planetary-gear linkage.

8. Automatic, 16mm, frame-by-frame photographing of each machine throw of the dice at the end of the cage pause in the upright position.

9. Nonresettable, mechanical, serial numbering of every half turn of the die cage.

10. Continuous exposure of one edge of every film frame via an auxiliary lens to reveal any lengthened time since the preceding frame.

11. Photographic proof (by manual insertion of a blank picture of the moving cage) that the decision to start recording was made before the first recorded fall of the dice.

12. 24-hour-a-day monitoring by a concealed Esterline-Angus operations recorder, showing every electrical stroke of the camera solenoid with a time resolution of five seconds.

13. All analytic procedures carried out by multiple paths with formal resolution of discrepancies.

14. Commercial microfilming of all hand-written data pages after punching their column-scores into IBM cards but before verifying those scores by transcribing individual die-face numbers from the photographic film.

15. Blind transcription and scoring of the photographic film records by a two-person team.

16. Clear delineation of the responsibilities of the experimenters. Data gathering was by the three experimenters, M, S, and P. Data analysis was done by M and S. Responsibility for planning and execution of data gathering, reduction, and analysis was retained by the author as senior experimenter. I planned all data forms, shared in all operations, closely supervised my assisting experimenters, and verified all analyses.

17. Complete protocols for data gathering and for every step of the analysis.

18. The serial prenumbering of data pages with a separate record of the assigned numbers.

19. As the experiment proceeded, the logged re-splicing of the

various measured lengths of chemically developed film into their original serially numbered reels, with a footage match to the manufacturer's norm usually to better than two percent.

20. Preservation of dice, camera, films, timing tapes, punch cards, IBM print-outs, and all original and derived hand-written sheets in an orderly fashion in locked cases.

Opportunities for Fraud

It is futile to attempt a logical proof that the data of an experiment were honestly gathered and analyzed, but it may be useful for an experimenter to describe the basis for his belief that he was not deceived. The principle most generally employed to minimize the possibility of falsification of records is that of time and space continuity. Continuity may be established by personal or mechanical surveillance. In the present work, as just indicated, interlocking mechanical systems of considerable complexity were employed to protect the gathering and storage of data.

The extensive routine precautions employed in this research cannot, of course, provide a guarantee against their circumvention, and indeed, may seem to the skeptic less important than the motivational constellation, technical capabilities, and the access to the data of each of the experimenters.

Kenneth Powell worked for me as a student assistant until the spring of 1951, first on an hourly-pay basis and then for a modest stipend. His principal duties were in the construction of vacuum-tube apparatus intended for the exploration of the extrasensory perception of time coincidences. Because of his gracious way of handling people, I asked him to help in the gathering of dice data in the present experiment. He tested about 25% of our subjects.

Ken recently reminded me that he was instructed by me at the time to avoid any concern with the statistical outcome of the experiment lest it affect his attitude toward his subjects. The records show that he served on the two-person film-reading team for about 25% of the transcribed data but was not otherwise involved in data reduction or analysis. He left the University of Pittsburgh in 1951 to accept industrial employment and later completed an M.A. in mathematics at this university.

Ruth Snowdon worked under my direction on statistical tasks I laid out for her. She was imbued with the need for precision and drove herself through grueling months of transcription and computation, with only the typing and criticizing of my endless letters and essays as entertaining relief. Her work was as accurate as that of any scientist I have known, including myself. However, she had no previous training in statistics or higher mathematics. Recently, in digging through my files I found that I had carefully recorded as of possible historical interest the fact that in 1953 she still did not know how to use the power-of-ten notation (i.e., she could not convert 10^{-2} into .01).

Personalities aside, it might be noted that the disappointing absence of a significant deviation from chance in the experiment as a whole, plus the partly unexpected nature of the discovered extra-chance effects (*See* McConnell & Clark, 1982) and their wide distribution—chronologically and among the experimenters—provide some assurance that these effects were not created by intentional mishandling of the data.

Perhaps the most that can be said regarding the integrity of the present experiment is this: It is my judgment that the psychokinetic effects found in the present data could not have been created by dishonesty, carelessness, or insanity by my co-experimenters or by any outside party. For obvious reasons, the other two experimenters are not in a position to make so comprehensive a statement.

THE MEANING OF PROBABILITY IN MULTIPLE ANALYSIS

When he tries to demonstrate the reality of a new phenomenon, the user of statistical method meets questions whose answers are not fully taught in the classroom. Preliminary to undertaking an analysis of variance upon the present body of data, I shall discuss one of those questions, namely, what interpretation should be placed upon a calculated probability value?

In a narrow sense the textbooks are clear enough. If a single analysis, planned independently of the observed data, is applied to an experiment and yields in a rigorous manner a null-hypothesis probability of .01, then the experimenter can properly say that in a long series of such experiments in which chance alone is operating, he would expect that a deviation from chance as great as, or greater than, that which was actually observed, would occur on an average of once in one hundred such experiments.

But suppose the analysis was planned while looking at the data and that several analyses were in fact tried, only one of which yielded a nominally significant probability figure? Toward this hypothetical situation one might adopt the attitude that analyses should never be done in this way, or one can recognize the probing, ever tentative nature of experimental science and attempt to deal with the matter in a rational, although nonrigorous, fashion.

To explain the second alternative, I shall begin by contrasting two extremes of statistical analytical activity: the testing of a precisely preformulated hypothesis, as against an undisciplined search for nonchance effects. Neither of these, be it noted, is close to the creative act of understanding nature.

If a hypothesis can be completely stated before an experiment is first tried, either the problem is trivial or the possible outcomes are circumscribed by an accepted theoretical framework. In either case the experiment itself is a routine technical exercise, even though its outcome may be of great importance.

At the other extreme, if a body of data is gathered for whatever reason, and analyses are applied without regard for pre-experiment expectations until a test is reached showing formal statistical significance, the experimenter can claim, at most, to be conducting an empirical investigation of the mathematical problem of the optional stopping of analysis.

Between these two extremes lies most of what is worthwhile as statistical investigation. For its interpretation, the experimenter must pick his way forward, guided by intuition, experience, and a wish to know reality regardless of damage to his preconceptions.

There are some helping rules that will be mentioned here insofar as they apply to the present data. How, for example, does one know whether to begin, and when to end, an exploratory analysis? And what kinds of analysis are most valuable?

For a given body of data the discovery of an anticipated experimental effect showing a chance probability that is significantly small is justification for originally unplanned further exploration of the same data. It is on that basis that an analysis of variance is undertaken here. The intrasession scoring decline in these data was one of two anticipated effects and, when originally evaluated by the "quarter-page distribution" method as dictated by precedent, the decline was found to be statistically significant (McConnell, Snowdon, & Powell, 1955a).

For exploratory purposes a variety of statistical techniques is available. One may choose a method of great formal generality, or a procedure specifically suggested by the structure of the experiment, or perhaps a test for nonrandomness whose special merit is its wide acceptance by statisticians. The analysis of variance, which I shall use, has all of these desirable characteristics.

In any exploratory analysis it is the purpose, as much as the technique, that determines the interpretation. A small probability obtained in asking a specific theoretical question is more suggestive of causation than the same probability would be if obtained in a wholly blind search for nonrandom effects. On the other hand, a probability that was calculated to assess a single, unexpectedly discovered trend in the data may be less convincing than one obtained in a systematic, preplanned search. In the latter case it may at least be possible to make a quantitative correction to probability values so as to allow for the number of tests that were tried. In general it can be said that, the more analyses one attempts, the less meaningful the resulting p-values, unless a pattern of significant probabilities emerges in the process.

When to abandon the exploration of data may be more puzzling than whether to begin. Among parapsychologists, even as among psychologists and sociologists, there are those who exercise caution in planning the formal analysis of an experiment lest a statistically significant finding be swamped by a host of chance probabilities. In this view, the ultimate skill in the analyst is to predict (fairly, of course, without peeking at the data) just what kind of computation will yield a small probability, while eschewing other tests of significance. To other experimenters it may seem that the guiding consideration ought to be simply whether the probable gain in knowledge by further analysis outweighs the cost in time.

Although in the present data the results of the earlier statistical analysis give assurance that an analysis of variance was justified, there will be questions of interpretation whose clarification may be helped by the preceding discussion.

Models under Test

The scoring decline effect, which was anticipated and found in these data, involves the patterns in which the data were gathered and recorded upon the data pages with all subjects and experimenters grouped together. The analysis of variance that will now be carried out is intended to explore for additional relationships among page patterns and the subjects or the experimenters. To do this, two models have been used, one relating page structure to subjects and one relating that structure to experimenters.

In the first model the score, X, obtained in any particular data column (of 24 dice) is assumed to be given by the equation:

$$X_{\text{SCHP}} = m + s + c + h + p + sc + sh + sp + ch + cp + hp$$
$$+ sch + scp + shp + chp + schp + r$$

where subscript s is the subject index, c is the index corresponding to one of the three columns within each half page of data, H is the index corresponding to the top or bottom half of each data page, and P is the index referring to one of the three pages of data gathered for each subject. The same letters in lower case are direct or interaction functions of the levels in the corresponding variables. These functions, when added algebraically to m (the observed mean for all scores) and r (the random error) are assumed to determine each observed value of X. Experimenters are ignored in this model, and the result is a $386 \times 3 \times 2 \times 3$ factorial experiment. The subjects are assumed randomly selected; the other variables have fixed levels. The data aggregated for analysis under this model are given in Table 1. Although X can have only integral values, it is treated as continuous variable without impairing the validity of the analysis.

In the second model the score in a data column is given by the equation:

$$X_{\text{ECHP}} = m + e + c + h + p + ec + eh + ep + ch + cp + hp$$
$$+ ech + ecp + ehp + chp + echp + r$$

where E is the index for experimenters (M, S, or P) and subjects are regarded as replications within experimenters. This gives a $3 \times 3 \times 2 \times 3$ factorial design, nonorthogonal but with proportional subclass numbers (since the number of subjects varies with the experimenter). All variable levels are assumed fixed. The appropriate data aggregations are given in Table 2.

Because the use of the target faces, one through six, was not balanced among the experimenters, there would, in principle, be a confounding between any dice bias and the main effect of experimenters. The matter is of no practical importance in these data because face use was approximately balanced, dice bias was small, and there was no significant experimenter main effect.

Because the expected significant finding in these analyses is for the linear component of the variance among the three columns of the data half-page, the column interactions are broken down into linear (L) and quadratic (Q) components.

Table 2
SUCCESSES (TARGET DIE FACES) OCCURRING IN EACH COLUMN POSITION OF THE
THREE DATA PAGES (EXPERIMENTERS SEPARATED).

Half Page	Page 1 (Cup-thrown)			Page 2 (Machine-thrown)			Page 3 (Machine-thrown)		
McConnell (171 subjects)									
Upper	670	683	702	687	685	669	719	710	678
Lower	664	660	674	678	616	661	673	700	666
Snowdon (128 subjects)									
Upper	528	469	473	505	528	525	550	540	504
Lower	508	504	488	537	495	503	531	528	476
Powell (87 subjects)									
Upper	374	357	369	361	372	330	367	316	336
Lower	340	356	350	357	364	345	388	338	335

Several supplementary analyses outside these two models are presented and discussed.

COMPUTATIONAL METHODS

The eighteen data-column target-hit scores (as counted and written down by the experimenter in each test session) were punched identically by an IBM "reproducing punch" into four punch-card decks (each having 386 cards) from a source deck containing one card per subject, which had been previously verified as described by McConnell, Snowdon, and Powell (1955a; 1955b). Sums of these scores representing the various needed column combinations were then cross-footed into these decks as space allowed, using an IBM "calculating punch." Sums and sums of squares were next printed by a digital computer using these decks. Mean squares were calculated on a desk calculator. All steps were verified internally and externally by a network of checks and independent repetitions designed to minimize in a logically comprehensive manner the possibility of undiscovered manipulational error.

In a separate operation, undertaken for other purposes and described below, all die faces were punched into cards, one card per half page of data per subject, and were machine-counted for targets (and nontargets), thus providing a completely independent verification of Table 1 totals, starting with the die-face data as originally hand recorded.

The mean squares and degrees of freedom associated with the several variables and their interactions are presented in Table 3,

Table 3

DICE DATA MAIN EFFECTS AND INTERACTIONS FOUND IN TWO FOUR-WAY ANOVAS OF DATA COLUMNS (C), HALF PAGES (H), AND PAGES (P), WITH EXPERIMENTERS (E) OR WITH SUBJECTS (S).

Source of Variation	Degrees of Freedom	Mean Square	p
E (Experimenters)	[2]	4.813	
S (Subjects)	385	3.7076	
C (Columns)	(2)	13.675	0.020 (1)
C_L (Linear)	1	26.902	0.005 (1)
C_L (Experimenter M)	(1)	0.819	0.63 (1)
C_L (Experimenter S)	(1)	23.503	0.009 (1)
C_L (Experimenter P)	(1)	14.257	0.044 (1)
C_Q (Quadratic)	1	0.449	
H (Half pages)	1	10.648	
P (Pages)	2	4.013	
E × C	(4)	3.020	
E × C_L	[2]	5.838	
E × C_Q	[2]	0.202	
E × H	[2]	2.521	
E × P	[4]	6.438	
S × C	(770)	3.2271	
S × C_L	385	3.3165	
S × C_Q	385	3.1377	
S × H	385	3.6861	
S × P	770	3.3886	
C × H	(2)	0.0235	0.007 (2)
C_L × H	1	0.0019	0.019 (2)
C_L × H (E_M)	(1)	0.082	
C_L × H (E_S)	(1)	0.510	
C_L × H (E_P)	(1)	0.138	
C_Q × H	1	0.0450	0.091 (2)
C × P	(4)	3.982	
C_L × P	2	7.125	
C_Q × P	2	0.838	
H × P	2	0.0779	0.022 (2)
H × P (E_M)	(2)	0.209	
H × P (E_S)	(2)	2.610	
H × P (E_P)	(2)	4.465	

Table 3 (continued)

Source of Variation	Degrees of Freedom	Mean Square	p
E × C × H	(4)	0.748	
E × C$_L$ × H	[2]	0.364	
E × C$_Q$ × H	[2]	1.131	
E × C × P	(8)	5.295	
E × C$_L$ × P	[4]	2.966	
E × C$_Q$ × P	[4]	7.625	
E × H × P	[4]	3.603	
S × C × H	(770)	3.6504	
S × C$_L$ × H	385	3.9258	
S × C$_Q$ × H	385	3.3751	
S × C × P	(1540)	3.3428	
S × C$_L$ × P	770	3.3672	
S × C$_Q$ × P	770	3.3534	
S × H × P	770	3.3442	
C × H × P	(4)	4.103	
C$_L$ × H × P	2	0.630	
C$_Q$ × H × P	2	7.577	
E × C × H × P	[8]	1.711	
S × C × H × P	1540	3.5777	0.023 (3)
2d + 3d order interactions	(4624)	3.4790	0.019 (3)
All but C	(6945)	3.4647	0.011 (3)
All but C (E$_M$)	(3075)	3.4724	
All but C (E$_S$)	(2301)	3.4264	
All but C (E$_P$)	(1563)	3.5053	
Mean (from $p = \frac{1}{6}$)	(1)	0.360	
npq (24 dice, $p = \frac{1}{6}$)	(inf.)	3.3333	
Total (experimenters)	[36]	3.4986	
Total (sans experimenters)	6947	3.4676	

Notes:
(1) Denominator = "All but C."
(2) Probability of so small a mean square. Numerator d.f. = 4624.
(3) Denominator d.f. = infinity.

along with probability values less than .05 or otherwise of interest. The denominator variances used in the variance ratios are those appropriate to the model under test. The components of variance associated with the third-order interactions were assumed zero. The corresponding mean squares then provided initial estimates of the error variance, to which the second-order interactions were compared. Probabilities shown in the table correspond to the long tail of the variance-ratio distribution, following the practice of Fisher and Yates [1953].

STATISTICAL FINDINGS

The mean-square of the variation, C, among the three columns of the composite half page has a probability of .020. The linear component (C_L) of this variation, i.e., the difference between the first and third columns, shows a probability of .005. Because die throwing was interrupted only at the end of every half page, C_L is the appropriate psychological measure of the decline effect, although for reasons of literature precedence the calculation presented in the initial report (McConnell, Snowdon, & Powell, 1955a) was made a little differently, namely, by the "quarter-page distribution" method.

The decline effect, C_L, was computed independently for each of the experimenters, M, S, and P, and found to have probabilities of .63, .009, .044, respectively. Thus, for two out of three of the experimenters the strength of the decline effect exceeded the .05 probability significance level. For the other experimenter, M, there was a nonchance effect that will be described in a companion paper (McConnell & Clark, 1982). Thus, the evidence suggests that nonchance die behavior, dependent upon the subject-to-subject sequence of target numbers, occurred for each of the experimenters separately.

The residual variance of the experiment, as shown by each of its several estimates in Table 3, is slightly but significantly greater than 3.3333 (the theoretical binomial variance corresponding to 24 die faces and $p = 1/6$). The analysis of variance cannot tell us whether this excess variability in individual column scores is the result of (1) a third-order interaction (assumed zero in the analysis), (2) bias among the several die faces (i.e., intrinsic p-values departing slightly from 1/6), or (3) uncontrolled psychological variables affecting the expression of psychokinesis. The matter will be pursued in the paper to follow (McConnell & Clark, 1982).

TWO SMALL INTERACTIONS: C × H AND H × P

Humphreys (1956) pointed to an interesting feature of these data when they were presented in the initial report (McConnell, Snowdon, and Powell, 1955a; 1955b), namely, that the mean squares associated with the interactions, column-by-half-page and half-page-by-page (shown in Table 3), are unusually small.[2] Humphreys regarded this unanticipated finding as cause for suspicion concerning the data in their entirety. His criticism, which included other matters of lesser interest, has been discussed as a whole elsewhere (McConnell, 1958). I shall concern myself now only with these interactions, which I shall analyze thoroughly.

These two components of variance have nominal probabilities only slightly larger than the probability of the sought-for decline effect, C_L. For these effects, taken jointly, there would seem to be three interpretations worthy of consideration. (1) Perhaps all of these supposed effects, including the decline, are of chance origin and without scientific or experimental meaning. (2) Perhaps the decline effect is meaningful but the interaction effects are chance fluctuations. (3) Perhaps both kinds of effects have a causal explanation.

The possibility that the decline effect observed in these data ($p = .005$) is a chance fluctuation from mathematical expectation must, of course, be granted. I wish to compare the second and third possibilities. In the light of somewhat more information than was initially available to Humphreys, I shall conclude that the most reasonable interpretation of the data is (2) above, namely, that the decline effect is meaningful but that these interactions are of chance origin.

The question is an important one. If the interaction effects are real, they must be explained. They are not part of any known psychokinetic effect. If real, they might reasonably be assumed to result from an undiscovered systematic experimental error. Could not the same unknown systematic error explain the decline effect?

The question can be sharpened by noting that what needs to be explained, as far as the interactions are concerned, is a variance that is too small rather than too large—excessive regularity rather than excessive variation. The decline effect, on the other hand, represents a variance excess. It is known that in some statistical situations the creation of an excess variance in one category at the

---

2. The mean squares shown in Table 3 are not in close agreement with those shown in Humphreys (1956) Table 1. The explanation lies in the fact that our initial report of these data included all 393 subjects, whereas the analyses of the present report are based on 386 subjects. As mentioned above, the seven subjects who asked for a change of target number during their experimental session have been omitted in the present analysis.

expense of another category can be accomplished by a selective interchange of data. Hence, if we suppose that the interaction and decline are spurious, causally-related effects, we might look for a data-exchange mechanism capable of creating both.

In my effort to assess these unexpectedly small interactions, I shall proceed by two paths. I shall examine the interactions in their own right to see what evidence they present of nonchance behavior, and I shall consider them in conjunction with the decline effect in a search for a possible interrelationship.

MATHEMATICAL INTERPRETATION

At the outset it should be made clear that the interaction probabilities cited by Humphreys are not directly comparable to the decline probability. The decline effect was specifically sought because it has been found by many past experimenters. Hence, the computed chance probability of its occurrence in this experiment may be taken at face value. The interaction effects, on the other hand, are the unexpected result of analytic exploration, and to their probabilities one must apply a discounting factor to allow for their selection from among the other, nonsignificant analyses.

For a correct intuitive grasp of the weight to be given to these interaction probabilities one must understand why they are an ad hoc finding and not even a part of the planned analysis of variance.

In the model, the mean square associated with the interaction $C \times H$, for example, is an estimate of

$$\sigma^2 + [SCHP/\{(C - 1)(H - 1)\}]\kappa_{CH}^2$$

where digit S is the number of subjects, etc., and where the omitted σ_{SCH}^2 is assumed zero on the basis of prior test. To compute the corresponding variance ratio, one divides this mean square by the best independent estimate of σ^2, and after referring to a table of probabilities, one infers that κ_{CH} is zero. However, in making this test, one notices that the numerator variance is unusually small. Even though κ_{CH} is zero, in the above expression the numerator mean square should still be large enough to estimate σ^2 with two degrees of freedom. How well it does so is measured by the *p*-value from the (single-tailed) test of homogeneity given in Table 3. To the extent that the interaction mean square is surprisingly small, one may question whether the mathematical model I have used is applicable to these data.

Using the prior estimate of σ associated with 4624 degrees of freedom in this experiment, I have found that two of the calculated mean squares (C × H and H × P), each associated with two degrees of freedom, are indeed small as estimates of σ^2. However, in carrying out this analysis of variance, I have surveyed a large number of mean squares, as shown in Table 3. It is not surprising that in two cases they were small enough to reach nominal significance. In ordinary statistical analysis one would discard these odd cases without concern.

But this is not ordinary research. The existence of a psychokinetic effect is generally doubted by scientists and even those who accept the phenomenon as empirically established have no theory to guide the interpretation of data. Indeed, the reason for this report is the need for a searching examination of all clues that may bear upon the reality and nature of the phenomenon. Therefore, it will be necessary to show by many ways, and in the most extreme detail, that these two small interactions can only be of chance origin.

EXPERIMENTAL MEANING

Let us consider next the experimental meaning of these interactions to determine how, if at all, they might relate to the decline effect. In the process of calculating the main effects and interactions of an analysis of variance, one aggregates the data in various ways. In Table 1, for example, the data are aggregated over subjects and experimenters. Thus, the number in each of the 18 tabular cells represents the total number of target die faces obtained by all 386 subjects in a particular column, half page, and page.

In order to calculate the C × H interaction, the data must be further aggregated by combining the three pages to give six score totals as shown in the top left section of Table 4. The corresponding aggregation for the H × P interaction is shown in the top right section of the same table.

The two interactions of interest can be examined structurally by taking the ratio of the upper half-page score to the lower half-page score in each column. This has been done in the table. For the C × H and H × P interactions respectively these ratios are 1.018, 1.022, 1.020 and 1.018, 1.023, 1.018.

That these ratios are all greater than the expected value of 1.000 is not important and, in any case, merely indicates a (statistically nonsignificant) scoring decline between the upper and lower half

Table 4

AGGREGATIONS FROM TABLES 1 AND 2 OF TARGET-HIT SCORES EXHIBITING
COLUMN × HALF-PAGE AND HALF-PAGE × PAGE ANOVA INTERACTIONS.

The interactions are small when the ratio of upper-half to lower-half score is
nearly the same (within one-half percent) for the three columns or for the three
pages, respectively. Note how these ratios vary by several percent (the chance-
expected range) when the data are divided by experimenter—thus implying that
the small interactions for experimenters combined are of chance origin.

Half pages and Their Ratios	C × H Column			H × P Page		
	1	2	3	1	2	3
Experimenters combined (386 subjects)						
Upper	4761	4660	4586	4625	4662	4720
Lower	4676	4561	4498	4544	4556	4635
Upper/Lower	1.018	1.022	1.020	1.018	1.023	1.018
McConnell (171 subjects)						
Upper	2076	2078	2049	2055	2041	2107
Lower	2015	1976	2001	1998	1955	2039
Upper/Lower	1.030	1.052	1.024	1.029	1.044	1.033
Snowdon (128 subjects)						
Upper	1583	1537	1502	1470	1558	1594
Lower	1576	1527	1467	1500	1535	1535
Upper/Lower	1.004	1.007	1.024	.980	1.015	1.038
Powell (87 subjects)						
Upper	1102	1045	1035	1100	1063	1019
Lower	1085	1058	1030	1046	1066	1061
Upper/Lower	1.016	.988	1.005	1.052	.997	.960

pages, which is an effect already established in the parapsychological literature. The smallness of the interaction mean squares that
we are investigating corresponds, instead, to the similarity of the
ratios within each group of three. The theoretical standard deviation for any one of these ratios is .019; the observed range of
variation is only .004 and .005 for the two groups. Had this range
been merely twice as great, there would have been no cause for
suspicion.

In order to observe the uniformities represented by these small interactions, one must aggregate the data in the particular ways shown in the top of Table 4. No other aggregations will do. For example, when one takes the same ratio without aggregation (upper score to lower score in Table 1) the results scatter by several percent in a clearly chance fashion, to wit: 1.040, .993, 1.021, .988, 1.075, 1.010, 1.028, 1.000, 1.028. Depending on how they are grouped (1–3; 4–6; 7–9 vs. 1,4,7; 2,5,8; 3,6,9), these ratios correspond to the $C \times H$ interactions for ANOVAs of pages separately or to the $H \times P$ interactions for ANOVAs of columns separately. They are, thus, "split-third reliability tests" of the data, and they fail to show the interaction effects. It follows that any meaningful creation of the questioned uniformities must depend upon the Table 4 aggregations of data, either actually or virtually.

In terms of the experimental protocol, these aggregations of data are highly artificial and could not occur except in handling the data. However, as I shall now show, in the recording of the data and in their subsequent processing, no combination whatsoever of data from the 18 separate column positions occurred up to the point of completing Table 1.

The data handling procedures have been described in detail elsewhere (McConnell, Snowdon, & Powell, 1955a; 1955b). The essential facts are these. In the original analysis, the *column scores* from the original handwritten data pages, i.e., the count of the target die faces occurring in the columns of each subject, were individually punched into IBM cards with separate card columns assigned to each of the 18 data-page column positions. The order of the card columns was the normal reading order of the entries of Table 1, with the understanding that all "Page 1" entries precede all "Page 2" entries, etc.

In one procedure, the frequency function of column scores was determined using a then state-of-the-art IBM "sorter-counter," in which the scores in one card column were counted with each passage of the card deck. The total scores were computed by a desk calculator as the first moment of the resulting score frequency functions. In another, separate procedure, the same results were obtained by adding on an IBM "accounting machine" the scores punched in the cards.

In a later, independent analysis, as already mentioned, the individual *die-face numbers* were punched from the original data pages into one card for each half page of data. These cards were first sorted by half page and by target number and then tabulated on an IBM "statistical machine."

The methods of these independent analyses from the original data pages ensure that no aggregation of data corresponding to the C × H and H ×P interactions occurred in the preparation of Table 1.

Because of these procedures, I can conceive of no way by which the interaction regularities could have been causally generated, either independently or as a concomitant of the decline effect, and regardless of whether the latter was created accidentally or even by deliberate fraud. Under the circumstances I incline to the hypothesis that these unexpectedly small interactions are of chance origin.

This hypothesis is further supported by the fact that the regularities move into the chance-expected range when the aggregated data are separated by experimenter as shown in the lower parts of Table 4.

CHRONOLOGICAL ACCUMULATION

In a further effort to find any causation in these interaction patterns I have examined the chronological accumulation of an interaction throughout the experiment. For this purpose I have chosen the $C_L \times H$ interaction, i.e., the linear component of the C × H interaction. This is the component of interaction involving the same data columns that generate the significant decline C_L.

Moreover, as a one-degree-of-freedom component, $C_L \times H$ has the advantage for my present purpose that (like the decline, C_L) its mean square can be exactly expressed as a score of so many die faces.

The 3 × 2 aggregation in the top of Table 4 for the C × H interaction becomes, with the omission of column-2 data, a 2 × 2 table (in which the cells might be designated as *a, b, c, d*). Then the $C_L \times H$ interaction, expressed in target die-faces, is the difference of the diagonal sums $(a - b - c + d)$, while the decline C_L is the difference between the left and right hand cells $(a - b + c - d)$.

For both the interaction and decline, the chance-expected value is zero throughout the experiment and the accumulation of an effect can be graphed in an easily understood form. This has been done in Fig. 3, for which the successive subjects have been grouped by tens.

There are several features to be understood in comparing these

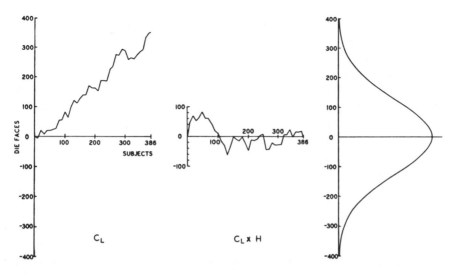

Figure 3. Chronological accumulation of the scoring-rate decline (C_L) and of the interaction ($C_L \times H$), for 386 subjects, computed after every ten subjects. Since these are single-degree-of-freedom components of variance and since the denominator of the variance ratio has a large number of degrees of freedom, they can be expressed directly in target die faces and their final values can be evaluated by visual inspection against the normal curve of error appropriate for the length of the experiment as shown. Although the final value of $C_L \times H$ is unusually small (-3 faces), it is apparent that this is the fortuitous result of the time of ending the experiment and that, taken over the course of the experiment, the $C_L \times H$ curve shows only chance fluctuations around its expected value of zero.

graphs. The final value of the decline, C_L, is $+353$ target die faces, which is significantly large with a chance probability of .005. The final value of the $C_L \times H$ interaction is -3 die faces, which is significantly small (in absolute value) with a chance probability of .019. In both graphs the accumulated deviation lies on the same normal distribution with a standard deviation of 126.7 die faces at the end of the experiment. This relationship is illustrated by the juxtaposition of a normal curve drawn to proper scale in Fig. 3.

The question of this unexpectedly small interaction falls into perspective from a study of this figure. The area corresponding to an end-of-experiment deviation so small that it has a chance probability of .05 or less, lies within a 7.9 target die faces of zero. In other words, a shift of 5 target hits in one of the four score-totals entering into this interaction could increase the apparent chance probability to more than .05; while a change of 3 faces in the opposite direction would send the probability to zero.[3] These same hypothetical changes in the data would, at most, be added to or subtracted from the decline score of 353 die faces and would have no important effect upon the decline probability. The numbers of die-face misreadings required to destroy the significance of these decline and interaction effects differ by an order of magnitude. In this sense the existence of a significantly large decline effect is essentially independent of the existence of a significantly small interaction, and, indeed, the latter is an analytical triviality.

As shown by the chronological curve, there is no consistent trend toward absolute smallness in the $C_L \times H$ interaction. The accumulating interaction score has wandered back and forth across zero expectation in a seemingly chance manner. Had the experiment been stopped a few subjects sooner the interaction would not have reached nominal significance while the decline score would have been affected scarcely at all.

Assuming that the decline C_L is of causal origin, the graph indicates the operation of the causal factor more or less throughout the experiment. In contrast, the interaction graph shows no evidence of persistent causation.

When, in the manner discussed earlier, the $C_L \times H$ score of -3 is separated by experimenters, M, S, P, the respective interaction scores are $+13$, -28, and $+12$ faces. None of these scores is suggestively significant by itself, nor do they show a trend when viewed as a collection.

On the basis of these analyses I conclude that the $C \times H$ and $H \times P$ interaction mean squares provide no substantial evidence of non-chance behavior.

DISCUSSION

No parapsychological experiment before or since this one has been burdened with such a panoply of controls. Nevertheless, the original report of this work was not accepted for publication until four years after it was first offered.[4] It was the adverse reaction to our findings by eminent physicists (with many of whom I had es-

---

3. It is obvious that an interaction score of zero must have a finite probability. The value, zero, arises by treating the discontinuous data as continuous.

4. The paper was not offered to parapsychological journals.

tablished professional rapport at the M.I.T. Radiation Laboratory in World War II) and the irrational reasons given by editors for rejecting our report that led me to conclude that the scientific leaders of our time would not competently examine empirical evidence for phenomena that do not fit their preconceptions of what is possible.

The scientific mystery of psi phenomena lies, not in their occurrence—they are commonplace throughout history—but in their a priori rejection by Western science. Thus, my course was set a quarter century ago: not merely to try to add to the already overwhelming evidence for psi phenomena but also to attempt to understand and to affect the belief processes of scientists. Understanding, I now feel I have gathered in good measure. That I have affected the beliefs of many scientists seems doubtful.

REFERENCES

Fisher, R. A., & Yates, F. (1953). *Statistical Tables for Biological, Agricultural, and Medical Research.* New York: Hafner Publishing (4th ed.).

Humphreys, L. G. (1956). Note on "Wishing with dice." *Journal of Experimental Psychology, 51,* 290–292.

McConnell, R. A. (1955). Remote night tests for PK. *Journal of the American Society for Psychical Research, 49,* 99–108.

McConnell, R. A. (1958). Further comment on "Wishing with dice." *Journal of Parapsychology, 22,* 210–216.

McConnell, R. A., & Clark, T. K. (1982). Progressive organization and ambivalence within the psychokinetic testing session. (Presented as Chapter 5 in this book.)

McConnell, R. A., Snowdon, R. J., & Powell, K. F. (1955a). Wishing with dice. *Journal of Experimental Psychology, 50,* 269–275.

McConnell, R. A., Snowdon, R. J., & Powell, K. F. (1955b). *Supplementary Information Concerning "Wishing with Dice."* Order Document No. ADI–4633 from Photoduplication Service, Library of Congress, Washington, DC, 20540, remitting $5.00 for photocopies.

5

PROGRESSIVE ORGANIZATION AND AMBIVALENCE WITHIN THE PSYCHOKINETIC TESTING SESSION

R. A. McConnell and T. K. Clark

ABSTRACT

The data-column scores from an automated dice-throwing experiment show a pattern of related trends involving mean score (the first moment of their frequency distribution) and their poorness-of-fit to the binomial distribution. The largest poorness-of-fit chi-square is found at the beginning of the testing session. *Within* the uninterrupted sequence of die throws (the three-column half page of data) a decreasing chi-square associates (from column to column) with a decline in mean score to below chance expectation. *Among* uninterrupted half-page sequences, a decreasing chi-square associates (from page to page) with an increasing first-column mean score. Moreover, the within-sequence scoring-decline effect increases over the testing session. Among the three experimenters, a low poorness-of-fit chi-square associates with positive overall deviation from chance and with strong scoring decline and vice versa. The authors conclude that these patterns show the existence of uncontrolled psychological variables affecting the emergence of psychokinesis and they postulate the operation of two, mutually multiplying factors, which they name "the organizing principle" and "the principle of ambivalence." They believe that these conceptions may lead to a unified explanation of scoring declines and "target missing."

SOURCE AND TREATMENT OF THE DATA

In a previous paper, McConnell (1982) re-examined the data from a die-throwing experiment and found an expected decline in the number of favorable faces obtained within sequences of throws as shown in Figure 1.

As described in the first report of this experiment (McConnell, Snowdon, and Powell, 1955a; 1955b), a pair of dice were thrown 36 times without interruption while the test subject wished for a particular die-face number to come up and the experimenter hand-recorded the actual faces as they occurred. The data from these 36 throws filled three columns, which followed one another, side by side, on the upper or lower half of the data page. This sequence was repeated six times in each testing session with brief intervening rest periods, thus filling three data pages.

The first-page dice were always thrown by the subject from a rough-lined cup, while the two succeeding pages were automati-

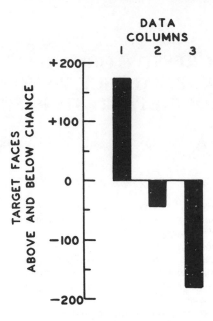

Figure 1. Decline in the number of favorable (i.e., target) faces obtained while wishing in an uninterrupted sequence of 36 throws of a pair of dice. As they were thrown, the fallen die faces were recorded in three columns of 12 throws on each half page of data. All half pages for all subjects have been combined in this figure. For each column the chance-expected number of favorable faces is 9264 ($p = 1/6$) and the observed standard error is 90. (This approximates the theoretical value of 87.9.)

cally thrown and photographed within a totally enclosing, motor-driven die cage operated by the experimenter. Data were gathered from 386 subjects, each participating in only one test session and using only one die-face target number (1 to 6).

When the 18 column-scores per subject were treated by analysis of variance in the previous paper, the linear component of the variance among the three columns on the half page was found to be significant with a chance probability of .005. This is mathematically closely equivalent to a t-test of the difference between the first and third columns of Figure 1, which is a customary way of evaluating a scoring decline in the literature of die-throwing experiments.

Analysis of variance is a method of partitioning the second moments of hierarchical distributions of data while ignoring the higher moments. In the present paper we shall examine the actual frequency distributions of scores of the data columns as they appear in the half pages of data, which may be more sensitive than ANOVA for the study of scoring fluctuations.

Decline versus Distribution

Ideally, the chance fall of a gaming die is a "binomial trial" with fixed probability of success ($p = 1/6$) for the on-top appearance of a prechosen face. If 24 such trials (one data column of 12 pair-throws in the present experiment) are grouped together, the relative frequency of target-face scores, ranging from 0 to 24, follows the binomial distribution given by the algebraic expansion of $(5/6 + 1/6)^{24}$. This is shown in Figure 2, where, for convenience, scores of 9 and above have been grouped.

The mean score and also the most frequent score of this distribution is 4. The variance, or second moment, of the distribution is precisely given by $npq = 10/3$, where $q = (1 - p)$ is the probability of failure and n is the number of trials. In the present paper the difference between actual distributions of column scores observed in this experiment and certain expected distributions similar to Figure 2 will be presented. These differential distributions will be evaluated against the chance hypothesis by "poorness-of-fit" chi-squares with 9 degrees of freedom.

The existence of the decline shown in Figure 1 will, of course, have its counterpart in the frequency distribution of column scores. To discover whether there was any other evidence of nonchance behavior of the dice in this experiment *in addition to* the decline in scoring rate, we calculated three different binomial distributions with trial probabilities corresponding to the observed number of target die faces in the three columns of Figure 1. These three expected distributions were averaged together and subtracted from the distribution of all observed column scores. The difference distribution is shown in Figure 3. By this procedure the resulting chi-square poorness-of-fit probability ($p = .001$) has been discounted for the decline effect which was shown in Figure 1. We may conclude that there is something happening in these data that is more complex than a simple decline in column scoring rate. (The above correction is the same whether one assumes the probability to be continuously declining or constant within each column.)

Recently, when preparing this paper for publication, we recognized that the variance of Figure 3 of the present paper corresponds exactly in the preceeding paper (McConnell, 1982) to the difference between the all-but-C sum of squares of Table 3 and the

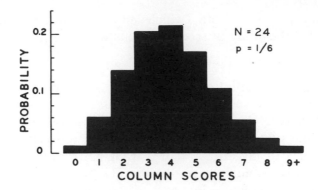

Figure 2. The theoretical probability of the chance occurrence of data-column scores, ranging from 0 to 24, that can result from throwing 24 die faces. A "column score" is obtained by counting the faces of one kind (corresponding to the subject's target number). The above figure is the so-called "binomial distribution" obtained by algebraic expansion of $(5/6 + 1/6)^{24}$. Later figures will show the observed deviations from distributions of this kind when wishing-for faces to match the target number.

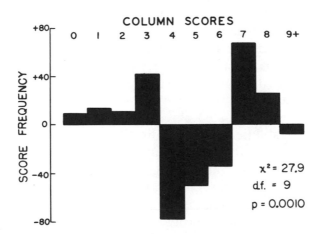

Figure 3. The deviation of the observed frequency of data-column scores (all columns combined) from an expected distribution computed to discount the decline displayed in Figure 1. The beyond-chance chi-square shows the presence of causation more complex than a simple column-to-column decline in the probability of a die-throw success. Total number of scores = 6948.

sum of three appropriate binomial variances, npq. This fact permits the following check of computational precision between that ANOVA study and the present target-score distribution study.

Using the ordinate values from which Figure 3 was plotted, we calculated the second moment of that distribution relative to the theoretical mean score, 4, and found it to be 1015.5. This needs a subtracted correction of 77.6 for grouping of the deficit of the 9-and-greater scores and another subtracted correction of .4 for the slight displacement of the grand mean from 4. Thus, the second moment of Figure 3 is 937.5.

The partitioned sum-of-squares associated with all-but-C in Table 3 of the previous paper is seen to be 24,062.3. The combined sum of squares for the three theoretical binomial variances, npq, based on the observed probabilities in each of the three columns of Figure 1 above can be calculated from Table 1 of the previous paper to be 23,125.5. The difference, corresponding to the second moment of Figure 3 above, is 936.8. The .7 discrepancy between this and the calculation of the preceeding paragraph is within the expected rounding error.

Excess Residual Variance

The previous paper of this dyad (McConnell, 1982) showed a statistically significant excess of residual variance compared to the theoretically expected value of 10/3 based on npq with $p = 1/6$. In the previous paper three possible explanations were suggested for this excess: (1) a third-order interaction of variables, (2) dice bias, or (3) uncontrolled psychological variables affecting the emergence of psychokinesis. We shall comment on each of these in turn.

1. The hypothesis of a third-order interaction involving column, half page, page, and subject or experimenter makes no psychological sense and can be put back on the shelf as unworthy of further attention.

2. The decline effect is self-controlled against fixed die bias, and in their original report McConnell, Snowdon, and Powell (1955a; 1955b) controlled against a hypothetical cyclic bias of unknown origin.

To explain the excess residual variance appearing in the ANOVA, we might assume a randomly variable dice bias. This would be a sterile hypothesis because it could not be experimentally examined and has no known, reasonable physical basis. In any case, although it might allow dismissal of the ANOVA finding of excess residual variance, it would provide no escape from the findings of the present paper.

All dice have some fixed bias, which presumably changes slowly with wear. In the pages ahead, several procedures will be followed to control against such fixed bias and to show that it is of no importance in the column-score distributions under investigation.

3. In the remainder of this paper we shall show how the excess residual variance of the ANOVA, as manifested in the poorness-of-fit of Figure 3, originates in unknown psychological mechanisms affecting the emergence of psychokinesis. That the mechanisms are psychological follows logically from two facts: that recording errors were controlled, and that the observed score effects appear in connection with the essentially random sequence of target-face numbers used in the experiment and, therefore, can have no meaning except in relation to the wishing of the subject and experimenter.

Although it is established by Figure 3 that the scoring decline and poorness-of-fit are statistically distinguishable effects, the question remains: Are they related? As a first step toward an answer, in Figure 4 we have separated the poorness-of-fit for each of the three columns of the aggregated half pages of data. The chi-square of Column 1 appears to be of particular interest.

CONTROLLING DICE BIAS

Each distribution of Figure 4 represents the difference between observed score frequencies and those predicted by a composite of 12 theoretical binomial distributions: six based on the observed frequencies of the faces, one to six, of the cup-thrown dice without regard to whether or not the face was a target when thrown, and six similarly for the machine dice, all weighted according to the use of cup vs. machine dice, and according to how many times each face number was used as a target when gathering the data. This controls against fixed dice bias.

Although this procedure has been carefully followed in Figures 4, 5, and 6, it should be mentioned that it is of no practical importance. Had the theoretical values, $p = 1/6$, been used in calculating these figures, in no score category would the difference have been greater than one die face and the changes in chi-squares would have been negligible.

As another, independent check against dice bias, pseudo-scores

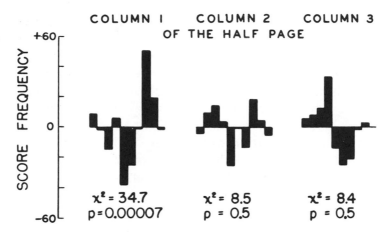

Figure 4. The deviations of the frequency of observed data-column scores (0 to 9+) from an expected distribution which was computed to offset any dice bias. In this figure all six half-pages per test subject are combined and each distribution applies to 2316 scores. From a comparison with Figure 1, it appears that poorness-of-fit accompanies positive scoring, while goodness-of-fit (small chi-square) associates with negative scoring, i.e., scoring opposed to the wishes of the subject. However, this is only partially true. From Figure 5 it will be evident that the poorness-of-fit *in Column 1* of the half page is *negatively* correlated with positive scoring.

(which were generated by scoring the observed die faces of Column 1 against their five nontarget face numbers) were plotted against the binomial distribution for $p = 1/6$ and the poorness-of-fit gave a probability of 0.3. These same data when scored for their true targets, yielded a probability of 10^{-4}.

And finally, aside from formal controls, it is hard to imagine how dice bias could create the chi-square patterns of Figures 4, 5, and 6.

HALF-PAGE PATTERN

The Column 1–3 distributions of Figure 4 are to be associated with the corresponding target-face-count bars of Figure 1. The first column of Figure 1 shows the desired psychokinetic effect, namely, an above-chance number of target die faces. The third column shows a reversal of that effect. The negative deviation bar is two standard deviations long and cannot reasonably be ignored. Why should the dice behave oppositely to the conscious desire of the subject and experimenter? Perhaps a clue will be found in Figure 4.

The method of construction of Figure 3, it will be recalled, was to subtract from the observed scores a theoretical distribution based on the three columns of Figure 1 so as to remove the decline effect. Figure 4, on the other hand, retains the decline effect fully and shows how it occurs in terms of column scores. In Column 1, the positive deviation of the column-score total (Figure 1) is accompanied by a highly extrachance distribution of scores, whose chi-square results mostly from an excess of 7s and 8s (Figure 4). (The 4s and 5s contribute little.) In Column 3, the same deviation of score total, but in the opposite direction, is generated by a very ordinary distribution of scores.

TESTING-SESSION PATTERN

Actually, the situation is more complex than might be supposed from Figures 1 and 4. The pattern of column-score distributions and score-total deviations is further explored in Figure 5, column by column and page by page. Like Figure 4, Figure 5 shows the difference between observed scores and a theoretical distribution adjusted to remove dice bias but retain the decline effect.

It will be helpful in understanding Figure 5 to bear in mind that the creation of a strong decline effect merely by a simple shift to a new die-face p-value may result in only a statistically inconsequential poorness-of-fit relative to the $p = 1/6$ distribution. Hence, decline and poorness-of-fit may be largely independent features in the same data.

In Figure 5 the decline effect grows from Page 1 to Page 3. Although not presented in the previous paper (McConnell, 1982), this growth, represented by the single-degree-of-freedom interaction ($C_L \times P_L$) in the ANOVA, is significant at the $p = .05$ level. As an isolated, post hoc observation, this growth could be dismissed as of chance origin, but as part of the pattern of Figure 5, it can be judged to be almost certainly causal.

In the occurrence of the poorness-of-fit chi-squares of Figure 5 the following features can be discerned. As in Figure 4, the interesting chi-squares occur in Column 1. The greatest chi-square occurs at the very beginning of the experiment, in Column 1 of Page 1. It decreases generally to the right, from column to column, and downward, from page to page. As the chi-square decreases from column to column, the desired psychokinetic effect decreases and then reverses. (This is seen most dramatically in Figures 1 and 4.)

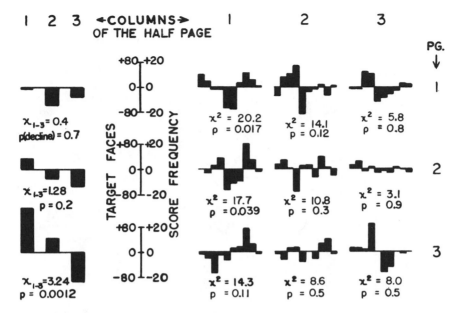

Figure 5. *On the right:* Data-column score frequencies as in Figure 4, but separated by page (with upper and lower half pages combined). *On the left:* The corresponding deviations of the target-face count from chance expectation, as in Figure 1.

As the poorness-of-fit chi-square decreases for Column 1, the Column 1 total score improves from page to page. Meanwhile, in Column 3, with no evident change in the poorness-of-fit chi-square the target-hit score grows negatively from page to page. (Chi for the scoring decline is the difference between the first- and third-column target face counts divided by the standard error of the difference. For each of the nine total-score deviation bars, the chance-expected number of favorable faces is 3088 based on $p = 1/6$.)

On the other hand, as the chi-square decreases from page to page (Figure 5, Column 1), psychokinesis "organizes itself" into a stronger positive score-total deviation in Column 1 and a stronger negative deviation in Column 3.

EXPERIMENTER INFLUENCE

In Figure 6, the data of Figures 1 and 4 are split by experimenter. The experimenter with the greatest chi-square has the weakest decline effect and a slightly negative total-score deviation; while the experimenter with the smallest chi-square has a strong

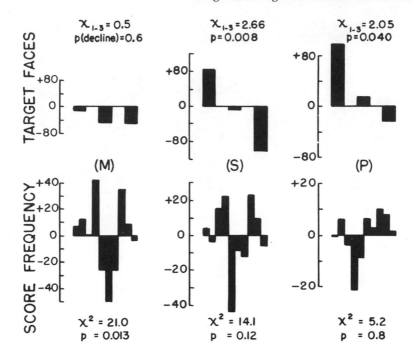

Figure 6. Similar to Figure 5, but separated by experimenter. The ordinate scales for both target-face count and score frequency have been adjusted for the different number of subjects per experimenter so as to show percentage changes equally. The numbers of subjects were: M(171), S(128), P(87). A countervailing trend, similar to that shown in Figure 5, is evident between poorness-of-fit and the strength of total-score effects.

decline and a slightly positive total deviation. (The latter fact may perhaps best be thought of as the result of a longer persistence of positive control before the reversal tendency dominates.) All three experimenters showed a psychokinetic effect, but it was best organized for P, and most poorly for M. The countervailing trends in poorness-of-fit chi-square and in mean scores are reminiscent of the column and page variations in Figure 5.[1]

---

1. It will be noticed that the probabilities shown in Figure 6 for the decline effect do not agree exactly with those shown in the ANOVA for each of the three experimenters. In the two papers the models under test are slightly different. In Figure 6 (and also in Figure 5) the decline chi-statistic with one degree of freedom is normally distributed and evaluates the difference between two means whose variances (calculated as *npq* from the observed numbers of target faces) are assumed to be known.

SUMMARY OF EFFECTS

Whatever its meaning, there is a pattern in these data that is of causal origin. It doubtless reflects the natural limitations that reduce psychokinesis from godlike omnipotence to an ordinary ability of the human mind. To focus attention upon the operational nature of the findings, we shall recapitulate the experiment and the pattern of its data in terms of their temporal elements.

Each test session lasted about 40 minutes and consisted of six identical sequences of events with a roughly two-minute rest period between sequences. Each sequence consisted of 36 controllable events (die-face pairs) spaced 8 seconds apart. Thus, each sequence of events lasted 4.8 minutes.

1. Psychokinesis was present and perhaps greatest at the beginning of the test session, although not well organized.

2. Psychokinesis was greatest in the first 12 events (1.6 minutes) of the uninterrupted sequence of 36 events.

3. Between events 13 and 24 (1.6 to 3.2 minutes) there was no evidence of psychokinesis.

4. In the final group of 12 events (3.2 to 4.8 minutes) psychokinesis reappeared but acted contrary to the wishing of the subject and experimenter.

5. An average two-minute rest period was enough to regenerate the decline pattern in which psychokinesis expressed itself.

6. Over the six sequences or cycles of testing (spanning about 40 minutes) psychokinesis expressed itself with increasing certainty both in conformity to the wishing (Column 1) and contrary to it (Column 3).

7. For one experimenter (M) the psychokinetic effect was present but erratic. For another (P) the effect was better controlled, giving a strong deviation in the first 1.6 minutes of the 4.8-minute sequence of events. The third experimenter (S) showed an intermediate situation. Thus, although all three experimenters obtained evidence of psychokinesis, there were differences in how it appeared.

The immediate questions raised by these findings would seem to be these:

1. Why does the control of dice reverse in sign after about 18 controllable events?

2. Why does the organization of psychokinesis improve as the sequence of test events is repeated several times within one testing session?

3. Why do some experimenters have better psychokinetic control than others?

Questions one and three are old questions, which the data of this experiment may sharpen. Question two is, we believe, a new question in the literature of parapsychology. It will be interesting to see whether the progressive organization effect can be found in other existing psychokinetic data.

Prologue to Interpretation

The purpose of experimentation is to guide further experiments toward the goal of eventual understanding. When pattern is discovered in data and its meaning is unknown, the experimenter is permitted, and perhaps obligated, to seek a hypothesis, i.e., to guess at an explanation in terms of relationships among generalized, nonobservable quantities.

In the present case, because of the subjective nature of our independent variable (wishing by the subject and experimenter, objectively determined by verbal instruction), we see no way to speculate except by using psychological ideas—a contingency for which our quantitative training has not prepared us.

In our attempt to make sense of the scoring trends of this experiment, we shall ignore the unknown role of the subject and assume that the experimenter was at least a co-agent in creating psychokinesis. As already indicated, we believe that the scoring pattern differences among the three experimenters are real even though we cannot compute a chance probability for those differences.

In the data patterns of this experiment we perceive the operation of two psychological principles as mutually multiplying factors. One of these we shall call "the organizing principle" and the other, "the principle of ambivalence."

The Organizing Principle

In our theorizing, the organizing principle has to do with clearing the mind and marshalling the attention of the psychokinetic agent. We surmise that the procedures within our testing session were such as to induce increasing order in the psychokinetic action. We suspect that this will occur progressively in any psychokinetic testing session of the kind we used.

Specifically, it is our hypothesis that the organizing principle manifests itself in a state of diminishing awareness, i.e., in an increasing state of mental dissociation. We prefer to describe this state simply as one of "passive alertness." It has been discussed in other language by professional psychics as a preparatory state for their performance. In parapsychological research it has been induced by the use of hypnotic procedures, progressive relaxation, sensory isolation, or the Ganzfeld (an environment of uniform sensory stimulation by noise and translucent blinders). We find it reasonable to suppose that the mental condition under consideration is similar to, or identical with, the contemplative state cultivated in the popular movement known as Transcendental Meditation and that it is an intermediate state in the psychological rituals of various Eastern philosophies.

In the present experiment the operation of the organizing principle was presumably encouraged by the simple, repetitive nature of the psychokinetic task and by the rhythmic turning of the motor-driven die cage. The absence of observers and the repeated act of calling and recording die-face digits may also have been important.

The evidence for the operation of the organizing principle in the present data (See Figures 4 and 5) is two-fold: (1) the inter-column and inter-page decreasing chi-square of the fit of the column scores to the chance-expected binomial distribution, and (2) the page-to-page increasing magnitude of the scoring-decline effect.

A large poorness-of-fit chi-square, when accompanied by a total-score deviation close to chance, may indicate erratic psychokinesis. For example, in the first column of the Page-1 column-score distributions of Figure 5 there is an excess of scores 7 and 8, balanced by an excess of 0 and 1 scores (where the score of 4 is chance expectation). Psychokinesis occurred, but it was unstable as to sign.

Had these 7 and 8 scores been created, instead, by "constant" psychokinesis (i.e., by a small constant psychokinetic shift in the target-face probability within the first column of Page 1), scores above 4 would have tended to be in excess, and scores below 4 would have tended to be in deficit. The resulting, hypothetical deviation in total score in that column might have been statistically significant, whereas, in fact, it was close to zero.

The force of this possibility can be seen by considering the total-score deviation and poorness-of-fit in the Page-3, first column of Figure 5, where a total-score deviation significant at the .01 level was achieved despite a poorness-of-fit chi-square smaller than in the Page-1 data.

Decreasing variability of data-block scores in the course of an experimental session is already known in the ESP literature. See, for example, the papers by Rogers and Carpenter (1966) and by Carpenter and Carpenter (1967). In the past this effect has been tacitly subsumed under the generalized idea of "decline." We believe that the target-scoring declines observed in extrasensory perception and psychokinesis reflect the operation of the ambivalence principle (to be described below) and that the decline in poorness-of-score-fit may involve an additional mechanism, which we have called progressive organization.

Our conceptions at this juncture are necessarily obscure. From the present data it cannot be said whether the organizing principle merely stabilizes psychokinesis or whether it allows "more of it" to occur. Nor is it apparent how best to account for the fact that, as the poorness-of-fit chi-square decreases from Column 1 to Column 3, the total score decreases; whereas the decrease in Column-1 chi-square from Page 1 to Page 3 accompanies an increase in total score. The nature of these ambiguities may be clearer after a discussion of the ambivalence principle.

We have searched without success for some model of learning that might reasonably be applied to the observed page-to-page increase in the decline effect. Perhaps others, more ingenious than we, will find something in published data or theory to make this a fruitful approach.

In our explanatory scheme, the data of the three experimenters all show psychokinesis but with varying degrees of organization, i.e., among these experimenters, when the poorness-of-score-fit chi-square is smaller, the decline effect is stronger (Figure 6).

If despite its limitations, our interpretation is essentially correct, then our data confirm the empirically well established idea that psi performance can be improved by short-term preparation for experimental testing by inducing a favorable state of dissociation.

It will be recalled that, in the present experiment, fitting each testing session into a 50-minute hour allowed, on the average, only about five minutes for experimenter and subject to get acquainted. Perhaps the first two pages of data per subject served as preparation for the more successful third page (Figure 5). If so, then a more adequate psychological preparation of the subject and experimenter before the throwing of the first dice might have resulted in a greater overall psychokinetic effect.

Alternatively, our findings suggest the following experimental possibility. Whereas, in most parapsychological experiments the effectiveness of psychological preparation can be inferred only by a comparison of results obtained with different preparational procedures, in the present experiment the progressive effect of preparation can be "watched" in the course of the experimental session. This direct exhibition of the effect of preparation might provide an efficient method for the testing of protocol variations.

THE PRINCIPLE OF AMBIVALENCE

The brain is coupled to, or exhibits, consciousness—we know not which. People, as conscious entities, engage in willing or wishing. We accept the fact that, when the brain has a conscious wish to do so, it can cause muscular motion of the body. However, as a result of many experiments similar in principle to the present one, it now appears that consciousness in its volitional aspect has access to another power which is capable of reconfiguring matter (e.g., controlling falling dice) without the intervention of the motor pathways of the brain. The exercise of this power has been called psychokinesis. As a practical matter, psychokinesis is so limited in scope that its occurrence is still in dispute among scientists outside the field of parapsychology.

According to the principle of ambivalence here proposed, the unknown causal train from conscious wish to the psychokinetic execution of that wish "passes through a dual channel" exercising affirmation and negation. These tend to balance each other and thus prevent the desired psychokinetic end result.

Under various circumstances the positive and negative tendencies may be temporarily out of balance so that either the desired result or its logical opposite occurs. (The nature of the "logical opposite" is presumably defined by the perception of the brain and not by absolute logic.)

It would appear that the effect of the ambivalence principle, unlike the effect of the organizing principle, cannot be controlled by dissociation techniques. It can, however, be manipulated by the structure of the experiment and doubtless in other ways.

In emotional terms, it is as though there is a balance between hope for, and fear of, psychokinetic success. Initially, in any segment of the testing session, after proper preparation, hope tends to dominate and a positive effect is achieved. As the effort of willing continues, the balance shifts from affirmation to negation. In some cases, the decline in average success may pass through the level of chance expectation and a reverse effect results, as in the present experiment. In general, it can be said that, as an empirical fact and for reasons entirely unknown, sustained volition tends to shift psychokinetic control from affirmation to negation even though, at a verbal level, volition remains presumptively constant.

The occurrence in the literature of inclined and U-shaped scoring curves, in addition to the more common declines, suggests to us that the balance of ambivalence is determined psychologically and not simply by physiological factors. This would not be surprising, since motivated behavior nearly always involves selecting between competing desires. On the other hand, at both neurological and behavioral levels, the concept of a dynamic balance between excitation and inhibition is frequently encountered in the explanatory literature of psychobiology and it is almost universally assumed that the brain necessarily must regulate opposing processes, whether they be psychological or physiological.

How a psychokinetic agent's knowledge of his scoring decline will affect the operation of the ambivalence principle is not yet known. It may depend upon whether that knowledge is merely a vague presumption from past experience or is obtained by immediate feedback from the end action (dice fall). Very likely, the effect of feedback will depend upon the personality of the agent.

We suspect that the manner of operation of the ambivalence principle is largely a matter of genetic endowment and that it can be correlated with personality traits, although we are not yet able to say how. Exceptionally psychic persons are presumably those for whom ambivalence is readily shifted in the direction of affirmation. Conversely, it may be supposed that there are "born losers" whose psychic ability tends to defeat their conscious ambitions—in gambling and perhaps in living, generally. The possible sociological importance of further investigation is apparent.

REFERENCES

Carpenter, James C., & Carpenter, Josephine C. (1967). Decline in variability of ESP scoring across a period of effort. *Journal of Parapsychology, 31,* 171–191.

McConnell, R. A. (1982). Wishing with dice revisited. (Presented as Chapter 4 in this book.)

McConnell, R. A., Snowdon, R. J., & Powell, K. F. (1955a). Wishing with dice. *Journal of Experimental Psychology, 50,* 269–275.

McConnell, R. A., Snowdon, R. J., & Powell, K. F. (1955b). *Supplementary Information Concerning "Wishing With Dice."* Order Document No. ADI–4633 from Photoduplication Service, Library of Congress, Washington, D.C. 20540, remitting $5.00 for photocopies.

Rogers, D. P., & Carpenter, James C. (1966). The decline of variance of ESP scores within a testing session. *Journal of Parapsychology, 30,* 141–150.

6

TWELVE YEARS OF GRADUATE STUDY IN PREPARATION FOR RESEARCH IN PARAPSYCHOLOGY

R. A. McConnell

Foreword

In 1982 we celebrate the centennial anniversary of the founding of the science of parapsychology in England. Let us take a backward look. Why, after a century of research, are psi phenomena not accepted by the leaders of science? In Chapter 3 we saw that the evidence for these phenomena is often not well presented. Could it be, also, that we simply do not have enough properly trained workers gathering professionally acceptable evidence?

Among its early members the Society for Psychical Research included some of the great scientists of the Victorian Age: Alfred Russel Wallace, William James, Pierre Janet, Charles Richet, Samuel Pierpont Langley, Heinrich Hertz. Two Nobel physicists, Lord Rayleigh and Sir J. J. Thomson, assisted in governing the Society. You will look in vain for scientists of that caliber in the membership of the Parapsychological Association today.

Despite great effort by a few investigators, it was fifty years before psi phenomena were partially domesticated for laboratory experimentation by J. B. Rhine at Duke University. By that time the age of scientific specialization was upon us and even Nobel Prize winners were content to tend their flowers within walled gardens. Any truly new field could expect no help from the rest of science.

This was the parapsychological milieu that I naively entered in 1947. Within five years, as I tried to publish my first research in journals outside of parapsychology,[1] I began to understand that there was enormous indifference and considerable opposition to parapsychological research from within psychology and physics, the two basic fields that should logically have a great interest in

---

1. The research reviewed in Chapter 4 of this book.

extrasensory perception and psychokinesis. Since that time I have
devoted myself primarily to investigating the sociology of science
in hope of bringing about a union between parapsychology and its
neighboring disciplines.

One of my long-held objectives has been to get competently
trained physicists and psychologists into parapsychology. How
might this be brought about?

It is a stark fact that competent people have no time to spare. A
few scientists from other fields might conceivably switch to parapsychology after their retirement in old age, but that would not
add much impetus to the research. To hope that a successful scientist will divert his attention from his own field in the full flower
of his career is unrealistic. So, likewise, is any expectation that a
doctoral candidate, after years of arduous training in some accepted speciality, will turn to parapsychology the day after the
degree is awarded. It is obvious that a personal commitment to
parapsychology, as to any other field of science, must normally be
made before the start of graduate study.

University students often ask how to get into parapsychology. I
always answer: You will need training at the doctor of philosophy
level, but you cannot earn a degree in parapsychology. Even to
allow you to try to do so would be unfair to you and to the
university. In a field without authorities, a doctoral examining
committee could not be confident that you had made "a significant
contribution to empirical knowledge"—which is the basic requirement for a doctorate in science. If, nevertheless, you somehow
obtained a degree in this subject, you could not make a living with
it. No one would hire a scientist certified only in parapsychology.
So, instead, you must get a doctoral degree in some field related to
parapsychology and, after you have successfully established a repu-
tation by postdoctoral research of an orthodox nature, you can
begin splitting your time between parapsychology and your area of
formal training. Such has invariably been my advice.

In my experience, this prospect of so long a road to travel has
always discouraged would-be parapsychologists who held, or expected soon to receive, a bachelor's degree. There was, however,
one exception. Many years ago a high-school science teacher
agreed to follow the prescribed road under my guidance. So begins
this cautionary tale.

Because any comment by me after you have read this account
would be anticlimactic, I shall tell student readers beforehand that

this case shows why it is impossible to become an accepted scientist in a nearby field if it is known in advance that you may later share your time with parapsychology. If that is your plan, you would be wise to keep it secret.

For those who are no longer students, my report may help explain why the phenomena of parapsychology are still rejected by our scientific leaders. It will illuminate the nature and depth of the opposition that this field arouses. And it will also explain, in part, why parapsychology has so few adequately trained workers and has therefore made little progress.

Most of the details of this case history are uninteresting in themselves, but they must be told, for otherwise the whole is unbelievable. What I have provided are authentic documents as they were submitted by me to the parties concerned, with no deletions or additions except as indicated.

I believe that the sequence of events related here could have happened anywhere and that, indeed, without its parapsychological overlay, it happens secretly every day in universities throughout the land. By circulating these documents privately and observing reactions, I have reluctantly concluded that about half of the competent scientists in our universities would behave similarly, given similar circumstances. This melancholy fact reflects the temper of our time and the nature of scientific research when it is practiced as an escape from reality.

MEMORANDUM OF 24 SEPTEMBER 1979

To: The University of Pittsburgh Interdisciplinary Committee for Psychological Physics: M. A. Lauffer (Chairman), R. S. Craig, A. E. Fisher, L. A. Jacobson, C. C. Li.

From: R. A. McConnell

Copy to: J. L. Rosenberg, Dean of the Faculty of the Arts and Sciences of the University of Pittsburgh.

Subject: Twelve years of graduate study in preparation for research in parapsychology.

Enclosures: Calendar of events relating to T. K. Clark's progress toward an interdisciplinary doctoral degree.

            Informational statement concerning the actions taken by T. K. Clark's Interdisciplinary Doctoral Committee on 14 December 1977 and on 11 April 1978, as submitted on 21 April 1978 to the Dean of the Faculty of the Arts and Sciences, together with its enclosure memo dated 15 October 1976.

            "The locus coeruleus in behavior regulation: Evidence for behavior-specific versus general involvement." *Behavioral and Neural Biology, 25* (1979), 271–300. [This journal-published paper is omitted from this presentation. It can be seen in any university biology library.]

It has been my privilege to serve as adviser or co-adviser to Thelma Kuzmen Clark throughout her 12 years of graduate study at the University of Pittsburgh. Now that she has completed all academic requirements for an interdisciplinary doctor of philosophy degree, it is appropriate that I summarize her experience for whatever value it may have for others.

Course Work

Mrs. Clark entered the University in September 1967 for the purpose of obtaining an interdisciplinary doctor of philosophy degree in biophysics and psychobiology in preparation for a research career in parapsychology. Upon my advice, she agreed to attempt no parapsychological research whatsoever until she had obtained her doctoral degree.

Although she was ready for graduate study in physical and biological science, she had no prior training in psychology. She was told that she could not expect to pass graduate-level courses in the Psychology Department unless she had the appropriate undergraduate background. Her first year at the University was spent obtaining the equivalent of a Bachelor of Science degree in psychology. In April 1968 she passed the Educational Testing Service *Advanced Graduate Record Examination in Psychology* at the 90th percentile against national norms for candidates seeking graduate school admission.

Mrs. Clark's next four years (1968–72) were devoted primarily to course work, including all the basic courses required or expected of a doctoral candidate in the Biophysics and Microbiology Department and in the Psychology Department. Ordinarily, in an interdisciplinary study program the student takes only a selection of the required courses from two departments. In Mrs. Clark's case, however, an administrative officer of the Psychology Department explained to me: "We don't like to see students slipping into our graduate program by the back door."

During the same period, Mrs. Clark suffered a series of illnesses and underwent a cholecystectomy. Because of this, as well as heavy family responsibilities, there were times prior to 1972 when her credit-hour load was somewhat lighter than is usual for a graduate student.

Experimental Research

In early 1972, Mrs. Clark asked Professor W whether she might do an interdisciplinary doctoral dissertation under his direction in the Psychology Department. He replied that he would not be willing to formalize such an arrangement until he knew that she was capable of doing laboratory research.

Mrs. Clark began experimental work under Professor W in April 1972. By the end of January 1973 it was evident that she had performed a successful pilot experiment and a statistically significant replication thereof.

With Professor W's endorsement, on 22 February 1973 Mrs. Clark filed with the University's Graduate Office an application for admission to an interdisciplinary doctoral degree program. Approval was granted in April 1973. Professor W of the Psychology Department became her Chief Adviser. As a faculty member of [what was then] the Biophysics and Microbiology Department, I became her Interdisciplinary Co-adviser.

The initial duty of such advisers is to determine the nature of the "Preliminary Examination" for the interdisciplinary doctoral degree. The doctoral Preliminary Examination (or "Preliminary Evaluation," as it is now called) is described on Page 25 of the University of Pittsburgh's *Graduate Programs Bulletin, 1977–1979* in this way: "Students are evaluated formally at the end of the first year of full residence. The purpose of this evaluation is to identify those students who may be expected to complete a doctoral program successfully."

Mrs. Clark had already been formally recommended to the Graduate Studies Office by two departments as having "the capability to complete an interdisciplinary program" (as required on Page 27 of the same *Bulletin*). She had passed the Ph.D. Preliminary Examination in Biophysics and Microbiology and the M.S. Comprehensive Examination in Psychology. I had been academic adviser for her first five years. Professor W had been research director for her sixth year. Her experimental work had been outstandingly successful. Presumably, her capabilities were well known. It was not clear what purpose would be served by a formal Preliminary Examination.

I wanted to certify Mrs. Clark at once as having passed the Preliminary Examination so that a Doctoral Committee could be appointed and she could advance toward her degree. In July 1973, three months after the establishment of her interdisciplinary status, Professor W decided that Mrs. Clark would have to submit a formal report of the research she had already completed before he would certify her passage. The significance of this requirement is to be found in the events that preceded and followed its imposition and in the nature of the research she was doing.

Earlier, in September 1972, the raw data from Mrs. Clark's completed pilot experiment had shown an exciting and important result that contradicted Professor W's theoretical expectation. By December 1972, raw data coming in from her first replication confirmed the existence of this anomaly, causing Professor W to revise a paper that was accepted for publication on 26 January 1973 (*Brain Research, 59,* 273–287).

In March 1973, shortly before Mrs. Clark's interdisciplinary status was formalized, Professor W required that she begin performing this experiment a third time to be sure of the result. In October 1973, he required her to begin a fourth performance. Each time, she obtained a statistically significant confirmation. He had no criticism of her procedure, but he could not believe the result.

For these and other reasons described below, it was not until 4 June 1975, more than two years after her admission to an interdisciplinary doctoral program, that Mrs. Clark was certified to have passed the Preliminary Examination and could request the appointment of a Doctoral Committee. At its second meeting on 11 November 1975, that Committee approved Mrs. Clark's dissertation research proposal and prescribed the form of her Comprehensive Examination.

Where the Research Time Went

After the Spring of 1973, Professor W had frequently expressed impatience with the rate of progress of Mrs. Clark's assigned tasks. For that reason, the use of her time in the 3½ years from April 1972 to November 1975 deserves close examination.

Each of the four performances of her first experiment required about 900 hours for data gathering and reduction. This was an unusually long experiment with rats, involving behavioral testing, brain surgery, histological study, and biochemical analysis. The data-gathering operations with the living animals were "time-locked," i.e., had to be done sequentially on a fixed schedule, so that if everything went perfectly—which it rarely did—the minimum possible time between experiments could be five months.

On 30 October 1972, six months after she began working for Professor W, Mrs. Clark was injured in an auto accident when her car was struck in the rear while stopped in traffic. In the resulting whiplash she sustained spinal nerve damage and internal head injuries affecting balance and vision. Over the next two years she was hospitalized for five weeks for diagnosis and therapy. As an outpatient she was treated in pain clinic for four months. She used a cervical collar and traction apparatus for a year.

Although her study of the scientific literature was interrupted for a year, Mrs. Clark refused to allow this accident to stop her research. She managed to keep up with the time-locked pace of data gathering and with the immediately essential parts of data reduction, but the preparation of the formal report (which, in July 1973, eight months after her accident, Professor W had decided to require for her Preliminary Examination) could not be seriously started until she had completed the four performances of her experiment in February 1974.

An analysis of her data records, which I did in 1975, covering her work in the years 1972–1974, showed that in response to her request for emergency technical assistance, four percent of her animal behavior sessions, five percent of her rat-brain lesioning, and 25 percent of the slicing and mounting of brains was done by technicians or other students.

Two other interruptions in the research period before November 1975 were (1) the preparation of a paper for *Science* (*190*, 169–171), which was undertaken at Professor W's request in the Winter Term of 1975, and (2) the execution of a supplementary, 60-rat experiment for Professor W, which began in March 1975 and took more than six months. With regard to the former, not only was Mrs. Clark involved in deciding what was to be said in the *Science* paper, but the mechanics of manuscript preparation and transmission were entirely her responsibility. The supplementary experiment just referred to was a partially successful exploration of some ideas of her Chief Adviser and a fifth successful performance of her first experiment. It appears in her dissertation as experiment No. 6.

Unrealized Alternatives

If Professor W had allowed a Doctoral Committee to be appointed in April 1973, after Mrs. Clark had spent a year performing and replicating her initial experiment and thereby proving her laboratory competence, the material published in *Science* in 1975 could, with variations, have been her doctoral dissertation.

Alternatively, had Professor W so recommended to her Doctoral Committee at its first meeting in July 1975, it could have accepted as her dissertation the experimental work she completed after the work he had agreed in 1973 to accept for her Preliminary Examination. That subsequent work consisted of (1) the broadening of the initial findings by positional variations in the surgery, (2) the results of the histological mapping, which she did not begin until March 1973, and (3) the biochemical analyses, for which the data were not available until 1974.

Instead, when the Doctoral Committee convened for the first

time in July 1975, although Mrs. Clark was eight years into her graduate program, it was decided by the Committee under the guidance of Professor W that, despite the importance and extent of the research already performed and accepted for publication in *Science,* an additional experiment using a substantially different technique would be required to complete her doctoral dissertation. Her detailed proposal for this new research was approved by the Doctoral Committee at its second meeting in November 1975.

At this second meeting, Mrs. Clark's Committee also assigned to her, as a task for her doctoral "Comprehensive Examination," the preparation of a written review of certain experimental literature peripheral to her area of research.

In November 1975, with Dr. W's encouragement, Mrs. Clark began at once her assigned laboratory work and completed the experimental phase of her doctoral research in October 1976. Again, her experimental work, although brilliantly executed, yielded results contradictory to the theoretical expectations of some of her Committee members.

The First Examination Task

In October 1976, Mrs. Clark turned her attention primarily to the Comprehensive Examination task assigned by her Committee. Because no minutes had been taken at the November 1975 meeting of the Committee, she prepared and sent to the Committee on 15 October 1976 a memorandum describing precisely her understanding of what was expected of her for the Comprehensive Examination task. Briefly, she was to survey the literature relating seven kinds of behavior to every kind of direct experimental intervention in a particular neuronal system in the pons and midbrain of mammals. This memo was accepted by the Committee members without comment. [It is included as an appendix in this presentation.]

On 30 November 1977 Mrs. Clark delivered her Comprehensive Examination paper to her Committee. Her formal oral examination on it was scheduled for 14 December. When she arrived at the examination room, she was told to retire briefly while the Committee "set the ground rules."

Ninety minutes later the Committee adjourned, asking me to take to Mrs. Clark the information that the Committee (with only my dissenting vote) had decided that, although the submitted paper [which came to 50 pages plus references] fulfilled all the specific requirements of the Committee, it could not serve as the basis for an oral examination of her comprehensive understanding of her field.

The difficulty was that, in covering the topics requested by the Committee within the page limitation imposed by the Committee, Mrs. Clark had compressed her treatment to the point where, in the opinion of a majority of the Committee, it was lacking in depth.

Mrs. Clark was given three months in which to write another paper to cover only one or two of the seven behavioral topics originally requested by the Committee.

It is interesting in this connection that one member of the Committee, who voted with the majority at this meeting, had previously told Mrs. Clark that he would accept her paper. He had returned to her his copy (now in her possession) on which he had written: "A thorough, well-written review except for minor points where clarification is needed."

The Second Examination Task

Mrs. Clark prepared a second Comprehensive Examination paper in which she reached the same theoretical conclusion as in the first paper but limited the scope of the evidence she examined, while including details she had been forced to omit for lack of space in the first paper.

On 11 April 1978 the Committee examined Mrs. Clark orally on her second Comprehensive Examination paper. The majority of the Committee decided that she did so poorly that she should fail but that they would give her a "charity pass" and allow her to complete her doctoral degree in view of the many years she had spent at the University. It was explicitly stated that she must be told that she would never receive a recommendation for research employment from members of the Committee (myself excluded).

It is perhaps relevant that Mrs. Clark's second Comprehensive Examination paper was published with only minor changes in March 1979 by *Behavioral and Neural Biology* (*25*, 271–300), a highly regarded journal of the Academic Press Corporation and one of the standard outlets for psychobiological research. She has since received over 300 reprint requests for this paper from 29 countries.

This publication of a major review article written by a beginning scientist who had only one previous scientific publication (*Science, 190,* 169–171) is in itself a recognition of excellence. The publication of literature review papers in neuroscience, as in most of the active areas of the natural sciences, is a privilege ordinarily reserved by editors for scientists with well-established reputations. In the present case, acceptance for publication is all the more a tribute to the originality and importance of Mrs. Clark's paper because she acknowledges on its first page that her review covers from a different point of view the same ground as a recent review by two well known scientists writing in *Progress in Neurobiology.*

Final Formalities

I have enclosed herewith: a calendar for the ready comprehension of the dates mentioned in connection with Mrs. Clark's graduate student career; an "Informational Statement" prepared by me concerning the actions taken by Mrs. Clark's Interdisciplinary Doctoral Committee on 14 December 1977 and 11 April 1978 and submitted by me to Dean J. L. Rosenberg of the Faculty of the Arts and Sciences on 21 April 1978; and a reprint of Mrs. Clark's second Comprehensive Examination paper as published. [The last of these enclosures is omitted in this presentation. The paper can be seen in any university biological library.]

After a meeting on 19 May 1978 with me and the Associate Dean for Graduate Studies, the Dean of the Faculty of the Arts and Sciences referred the matter to the Associate Dean. Mrs. Clark then formally requested changes in the membership of her Doctoral Committee and an extension of time under the statute of limitations to allow her to complete her degree.

The Associate Dean reported to me that, in response to a request for a recommendation on the matter of the extension of time, Professor W said that a month should suffice for Mrs. Clark to write her dissertation. This estimate of the time to prepare a report covering four and one-half years of experimental research was too small by an order of magnitude. The most generous explanation is that Professor W had no precise knowledge as to what data gathered under his direction had already been formally presented and what had been given only a preliminary evaluation.

Mrs. Clark's dissertation, *The Region of the Ascending Dorsal Noradrenaline Bundle of the Locus Coeruleus in Relation to Male Rate Copulatory Behavior* (81 pages of text, 10 tables, 13 figures, and 20 pages of references), was accepted without change by the revised examining committee on 13 June 1979. It ranks among the finest doctoral dissertations produced at the University of Pittsburgh. [Copies are available from University Microfilms International, Catalog No. 80–15294. Those findings from the dissertation that had not previously been presented in *Science* have since been published by Dr. Clark as sole author in *Brain Research, 202* (1980), 429–443.]

UPDATED CALENDAR OF EVENTS
RELATING TO T. K. CLARK'S PROGRESS
TOWARD AN INTERDISCIPLINARY DOCTORAL DEGREE

Entered the University of Pittsburgh as a graduate
student .... Sept. 1967

First year spent in undergraduate study in psychology. Passed the E.T.S. *Advanced Graduate
Record Examination in Psychology* at the 90th
percentile .... April 1968

Completed four years of graduate courses in Biophysics and Psychology with a final grade average of 3.4 on the scale 0–4 .... April 1972

Began research under Dr. W .... April 1972

Completion of pilot experiment and first
repetition .... March 1973

Start of a supplementary experiment requiring six
months for data gathering and reduction .... March 1975

Acceptance of paper by *Science* (*190*, 169–171)
covering four successful performances of first
experiment, each performance requiring six
months for data gathering and reduction .... May 1975

First meeting of T. K. Clark's Doctoral Committee, at which it reviewed her credentials and
formulated the remainder of her graduate
program .... 15 July 1975

Second meeting of T. K. Clark's Committee, at
which it approved her dissertation proposal
and specified her Comprehensive
Examination .... 11 Nov. 1975

Completion of all laboratory work for the doctoral
dissertation .... Oct. 1976

Memo sent by T. K. Clark to her Committee, de-
lineating the Committee's Comprehensive Examination requirement. (Included as an appendix to this presentation.) .... 15 Oct. 1976

Memo sent by R. A. McConnell to Dr. W, with
 copies to the Committee, summarizing the
 Committee's Comprehensive Examination
 requirement .... 11 April 1977

Memo sent by T. K. Clark to her Committee, sub-
 mitting an outline of her Comprehensive Examination review paper and its bibliography . 23 June 1977

Submission by T. K. Clark to Dr. W (her chief
 adviser) and to R. A. McConnell (her co-
 adviser) of a draft of the "Introduction" and
 of the surveys for three of the seven behaviors
 to be covered in the Comprehensive Examination review paper .... 8 Sept. 1977

Delivery of her Comprehensive Examination review paper by T. K. Clark to the Committee
 members .... 30 Nov. 1977

Rejection of T. K. Clark's Comprehensive Examination paper by the Committee in executive
 session without examining her .... 14 Dec. 1977

The comprehensive examination of T. K. Clark by
 her Committee after the preparation of a second examination paper .... 11 April 1978

Publication by T. K. Clark of her second Comprehensive Examination review paper in *Behavioral and Neural Biology* (*25*, 271–300) .... March 1979

Defense of doctoral dissertation .... 13 June 1979

Publication by T. K. Clark in *Brain Research* (*202*,
 429–443) of a second experimental paper
 based on her dissertation research .... Dec. 1980

Informational Statement
Concerning the Actions Taken by
T. K. Clark's Interdisciplinary Doctoral Committee
on 14 December 1977 and on 11 April 1978

As Prepared by R. A. McConnell
and Submitted on 21 April 1978 to the Dean of the Faculty
of the Arts and Sciences of the University of Pittsburgh

Table of Contents of Informational Statement

Specification of the Comprehensive Examination Task

At its second meeting on 11 November 1975, C's Interdisciplinary Doctoral Committee approved her doctoral research proposal and specified a survey of a certain area of the scientific literature to fulfill her Comprehensive Examination requirement. No minutes were taken at this meeting.

For reasons of experimental continuity, C finished her dissertation research in October 1976 before beginning her Comprehensive Examination survey.

To remove as far as possible any ambiguity before beginning the survey, C sent to the Committee a memo, dated 15 October 1976 (submitted herewith), defining her understanding of her task. This memo was accepted without comment by her Committee members and, together with a subsequently imposed 20 or 40 typewritten-page length limit, governed the writing of her survey.

Her instructions were to survey for all mammals the literature relating behavioral observation to direct experimental intervention in the brain at the site of the nucleus locus coeruleus and its dorsal noradrenaline bundle of axons. To this end, she searched the literature and collected about 500 papers, perhaps half of which eventually required careful study. Her examination survey, as submitted to her Committee, cited 168 papers, about 110 of which were experimental reports directly relevant to her task. The remainder were for background.

The literature of six of the seven kinds of behavior to be surveyed was new to C. Each "behavior" (e.g., learning, locomotion, sleep) has its own concepts and measuring techniques. Starting from a state of ignorance, she mastered these specialties in depth. She prepared herself to make independent judgments that she could defend against experts from each area.

The entire operation, beginning with the search for papers and ending with the preparation of a fifty-page summary of her findings (the text of her Comprehensive Examination survey), took about 2000 hours, which I regard as a reasonable length of time for the assigned task—although far too long for a Comprehensive Examination paper.

Rejection by the Doctoral Committee on 14 December 1977

On 30 November 1977, C delivered her completed Comprehensive Examination survey to her Interdisciplinary Doctoral Committee with a request that a meeting be called to examine her. Her transmitting memo and the fifty-page survey are submitted herewith. [Omitted from this presentation.]

That Committee meeting, the first since 11 November 1975, was held on 14 December 1977. C was asked to leave the room and was told that she would be called in after the Committee has "set the ground rules." She was not recalled, but, at the end of the meeting, I was asked to tell her of the Committee's action.

Dr. W, C's chief adviser and research director, made an introductory speech in which he said he found her paper unacceptable for the Comprehensive Examination and suggested that she be given a new task. This idea was endorsed by Drs. X and Y, with little participation by myself or Dr. Z. Evidently the rejection had been prearranged.

From the circumlocutions used, I inferred that C's paper was rejected because it was in some sense deficient in analysis. The following were the only specific criticisms that I remembered immediately following the meeting. "The paper is no more than an annotated bibliography." "It is something that might have been written by a science writer." "It sounds as though it was written by an outsider." "It could have been written by abstracting the abstracts."

Although it was not so stated, these comments amount to the accusation that C's paper is a mechanical collection of facts, put together without understanding. My opinion is that her paper is an essay whose main body consists of a careful selection of experimental conditions and findings, organized with skill and understanding into a form that was dictated by the nature of the assigned task and the constraints previously imposed by the Committee.

As an example of C's "unprofessional attitude," it was pointed out that the references to journal papers at the end of her paper had not been arranged in a single alphabetical list. (The references had, instead, been alphabetized by chapter and, in four cases, after consulting me, a supplemental list of alphabetized references had been inserted to save retyping costs. All pages had a fully identifying heading. All entries were accurately typed in conformity with the American Psychological Association standard. The entire arrangement was explained in one brief sentence and clearly indexed in the Table of Contents for the convenience of the reader. If there was any appreciable inconvenience to the Committee members, it was only because they failed to look first at the Table of Contents to discover the logic of the arrangement. Moreover, it should be remembered that this was not a paper submitted for publication but one submitted to the Committee as a basis for exploring the student's knowledge.)

Dr. W volunteered the statement that, in doing her survey, C had indeed fulfilled all of the specific requirements of the Committee. Then he added that this was meaningless because she had failed to grasp what was wanted. He went on to say that C was "too much concerned with memoranda and mere legalisms."

The Committee members opposing C's paper agreed that what they found most disturbing was, not that C had written this paper, but that she has submitted it in the belief that it was a *good* paper. This, they said, raised serious doubts in their minds as to whether she had the qualifications necessary to complete the doctoral degree.

[Having anticipated the possibility of committee antagonism,] I read a short, prepared statement to the effect that C had done a careful integration of more than 100 papers that met the selection criteria approved by the Committee and that I wished to report what I had learned of her methods.

I listed the technical factors by which she had evaluated each paper and described how she had tried to present selectively to the reader the important conditions and findings of each paper as evidence bearing upon the question she was investigating, namely, the existence of specialization at the level of behavior in the locus coeruleus system of the brain. I gave to each Committee member a sheet listing the dates on which C had taken each step in consultation with the Committee in preparing her paper. However, because a decision to reject her paper had been made before the meeting began, my words were without effect.

I was asked what C (age 47) intended to do with her degree. Did her husband (age 48) have a position that he could give up to follow her to another city? Did she think there were positions in the Pittsburgh area? The relevance of this interrogation to the business of the Committee was not apparent to me.

Dr. Z accepted without objection the viewpoint of the others, although on 6 December he had told C in person that he thought she had a good paper, that he had learned some interesting things from it, and that he would approve it. When I visited him on the day following the Committee meeting, he volunteered the information that he had told C earlier that he accepted her paper, but had changed his mind and agreed with the others as to the inadequacy of the paper because this was his first experience on a Comprehensive Examination committee and he had not realized that a more analytic approach was expected. He told me that C's paper seemed to be well organized and complete and that, after some improvement, should be quite publishable since nothing like it had been done before. In this connection, it should be noted that Dr. Z's area of scientific specialization is psychobiology, and his preferred experimental techniques are as close to those of the other three members of the Committee as theirs are to each other.

The Second Comprehensive Examination Assignment

It was said at the 14 December 1977 meeting that C's new task might cover only one or two behaviors instead of seven and that it must not be too long—15 to 20 pages should suffice. My inquiries and those of Dr. Z failed to elicit anything definite as to what more was wanted, but I got the impression that each Committee member had a somewhat different idea as to whether, and how much, there should be of behavioral theory, biochemical theory, inter-paper comparison, within-paper criticism, creative speculation, etc. When I attempted to press the point, I was told: "We can't tell her what to write. She must figure that out for herself." When I asked: "Do you mean that she should find some ideas and develop them?", there seemed to be consensual approval.

A time limit of two months was set for C to complete her second paper. This was changed to three months when I reminded the Committee that, unlike the rest of us, C maintains a home without outside domestic help and commutes by car 85 miles a day. At the end, I was told that C could come to each Committee member, who would be glad to discuss the task and perhaps make suggestions.

Later, after consulting individually with her Committee members, C began her new task. However, in view of the unexplained rejection of her first Comprehensive Examination survey, the peculiar vagueness of her new directive, and the range of research styles represented on her Committee, she had little confidence that she would be able to put together an acceptable paper, and she saw a real danger that, in attempting to do so, she might concoct a melange of such wide scope that she would be unable to defend it.

Prior Consultation by the Student with the Committee

At the 14 December meeting it was said that, if C had taken the trouble to consult with members of her Committee, she would not have submitted the kind of paper she did. The implication was that she did not consult with her Committee. I cannot reconcile this with the following facts.

To begin with, on several occasions the Committee considered, or was reminded of, its requirements and should have known what kind of paper was implied by those requirements. Those occasions were on 11 November 1975 at the second meeting of the Committee, when the original assignment was made; on 15 October 1976, when C personally delivered to each Committee member a memo (enclosed herewith) explicating the Committee's assignment; and on 11 April 1977, when I sent a memo to Dr. W, with a copy to each Committee member, in which I summarized what C was doing. [This last memo was attached to this statement when originally submitted but is omitted from this presentation.]

Subsequently, in June 1977, C delivered to each Committee member an outline of her intended survey and a preliminary list of the papers she expected to cover. She offered to, and did in fact, return in a few days to hear their comments and advice. [Her transmitting memo was originally enclosed with this statement but is omitted here.]

At that time, Dr. Y told her that her paper ought to be restricted to one or two behaviors and that he would not read more than 20 pages. Evidently, he was the only member of the Committee who was able to foresee, even at that late date, the magnitude of the task that had been given to C.

Dr. W, on the other hand, in June 1977, urged that C broaden the survey to include pharmacological studies, behavioral theory, and sexual-behavior literature from areas distant from the neurological system under investigation.

At the same time, Dr. Z suggested to C in writing (now in her file) that she include some behavior-lesioning experiments in the terminal areas of the axons of the system she was investigating. As C pointed out to me, had he thought a moment, he would have realized that this could include lesioning experiments from nearly all areas of the brain—a clearly impractical suggestion.

Thus, in June 1977, half way through the task, one Committee member was advocating a contracted coverage and two were asking for expansion. When C reported Dr. Y's ideas to Dr. W, he indicated in an offhand manner that there was no problem since the question had already been decided by the Committee and that she should move ahead. He wanted coverage of all behaviors.

In September 1977, C took a first draft of her "Introduction" and three of seven of the planned behavioral studies to Dr. W (as her chief adviser) and to me (as co-adviser). Dr. W marked and returned his copy. It is available for inspection and shows no major criticisms and no hint that the paper would be unacceptable in toto.

These facts appear to me to show a pattern of consultation by C rather than isolation. In retrospect, Dr. W may believe that C should have been consulting with him on a weekly basis, but he made no effort to have her do so and, in fact, he has always been rather inaccessible. On many occasions throughout her preceeding five and one-half years association with the Psychology Department, C had reported to me that she was receiving less than enthusiastic co-operation from Dr. W.

Events Immediately Subsequent to the 14 December Rejection

C had expected to be orally examined on her understanding of the papers she had covered in her survey, and she was disappointed that the Committee refused to question her. Because the body of her survey dealt primarily with only the results from research papers, they must have assumed that she had no knowledge in depth of those papers. This aspect of the Committee's action is of interest in the light of the following events.

On 16 December 1977, C visited Dr. Z to ascertain what he thought she ought to do to satisfy the Committee' requirement for a new paper. In the course of their conversation he asked questions about the meaning or explanation of experimental results she had surveyed in her paper. Several times he said some version of the following: "But, C, why didn't you say that in your paper? That's what the Committee wanted." To each such comment her answer was in effect: "Such discussion was irrelevant to the question I was investigating, and, moreover, there was not room for it within the space limitation I had been given."

Dr. Z said that whatever satisfied the rest of the Committee would undoubtedly satisfy him. He advised C to try to find out what Drs. W and X wanted. He returned his copy of her paper (now in her possession) with its marginal comments and queries. On the title page he had written: "A thorough, well-written review except for minor points where clarification is needed."

On 20 December 1977, C visited Dr. Y to get his advice on how to write her new paper. He had told her on 6 December (eight days before the Committee's rejection) that he had not yet read her survey but that he had scanned it and found it unacceptable because it was lacking in depth. This time, he interrogated her on the background of that survey, covering a range of papers from it—some to which she had devoted much space and some to which she had given only passing mention. He asked various questions and inquired especially as to why certain papers were good evidence or poor evidence for her thesis. At the end he commented as follows: "McConnell was right that you do know the papers. It is regrettable that you didn't show it in your writing—although we might have found out by an oral examination."

He also offered suggestions as to how she might write her next paper, and said that her difficulty was that she had "brought a memo to the Committee [the memo of 15 October 1976] and had then dropped into oblivion for a year"—a statement that does not conform to the facts I have cited above.

I visited Dr. Y on 3 January 1978 to get his ideas on C's situation. He said he had talked to her and that she knows the papers but she had not put it down in her writing. "She should have come around for advice." When I reminded him that she had taken a first draft of half of the paper to Dr. W in September, he said: "That's a hard point to respond to. I hadn't known about that until I saw the list of dates you handed out at the meeting." I told him that C still holds the first draft returned by Dr. W and that it contains no criticisms of any importance.

In describing to me what was wrong with C's paper, Dr. Y said that on 20 December 1977 he had asked her why she had given so little space to one paper as compared to another, and that, in response, she had explained to him in technical detail the weaknesses of those papers to which she had paid little attention. That, he said, was what she should have put into her paper.

When Dr. Y said to me that C should have been consulting all along, I said that Dr. W was a hard man to see. Dr. Y said he did not know how to interpret that. I replied that it would be generous to say that Dr. W had given C five hours of his time throughout all of the years she had been with him—not counting the several hours he had spent with her in the preparation of her *Science* paper. Dr. Y said that he (Dr. Y) gives almost that much time to each student each week. I went on to explain that everything C had learned in the way of technique she had learned from other graduate students (or technicians or post-doctoral fellows) and that, in the end, she was teaching other students.

I said that the only laboratory supervision she received came from me (or the person whose laboratory equipment she might have been using at the moment). When I saw that her experimental results were turning out contrary to Dr. W's expectations, I decided that, for her protection as well as my own, I would have to find out what she was doing. Even though it was not my line of research, I spent many hours observing her and asking questions while she worked in behavioral testing, in brain surgery, in histological analysis, and in biochemical assaying, and I independently re-analyzed a large block of her data.

When I suggested that Dr. W's lack of involvement could perhaps be understood since she is not "one of the boys," Dr. Y said he did not see how that could enter. He said she "has a pleasant way about her" and "is easy to get along with." Dr. Y evidently misunderstood my meaning.

The fact is, as shown by numerous incidents over the years, which were reported to me by C when they occurred, Dr. W, although he is by nature an easygoing and friendly person, never wanted C as a graduate student and, consciously or otherwise, frequently showed it.

On 21 December 1977, C visited Dr. W for the purpose of getting his instructions. He was solicitous and urged her to spend more time with the graduate students so that she could get some feeling for the research—a socially preposterous suggestion since C is ten years older than Dr. W, is no longer taking courses with graduate students, and is not currently engaged in laboratory work. He offered to get her a desk in his laboratory—evidently having forgotten that he had refused her request for a desk when she was doing her research several years earlier and needed it for the efficient integration of her work as well as for student contact.

C had a feeling that she was being talked to as a child. Dr. W's evident premise was that she was out of touch with the research. Everything she said was bent to fit his preconception that she had no appreciation of the literature of her field. In the course of discussing her rejected survey, she said: "Experiments are still being performed as though there is a one-to-one correspondence between structure and behavior." He responded: "I'm sorry to hear you say that. It shows that you don't know what we have been doing in this laboratory. It has been years since anyone in the field thought in terms of one structure: one behavior."

C responded: "You didn't hear what I said. I was referring, not to what experimenters *say,* but to what they *do.* I said: 'Experiments are still being *performed* as though there is a one-to-one relationship between structure and behavior.' "

Then she cited his own *Brain Research* paper (1973, *59,* 273–287) wherein, by lesioning in an area of the hypothalamus, the experimenters had displayed a relationship between noradrenaline depletion and copulatory deficit. "The point of my survey," she said, "was that I found no such relationship with the locus coeruleus." Dr. W seemed to hear her words and yet not to hear them— as though there were some barrier to his understanding.

To make her point, C might better have cited her own research, both stages of which were undertaken at Dr. W's (or the Committee's) direction with the expectation that a relationship between the locus coeruleus and sexual behavior might be found.

Dr. W did not on 21 December discuss details of any of the papers from the survey C had submitted. However, earlier, on 9 December 1977, when C had visited him to complete arrangements for the 14 December Committee meeting, he had discussed one of the papers with her (Jones et al., 1977), finding fault with her failure to treat pharmacological evidence generally in her survey. He said C had "violated her own no-pharmacology rule" by citing this author's conclusion, which was based upon pharmacological evidence. He evidently was still not satisfied that C had not expanded the scope of her survey to include pharmacological evidence generally. (See above, paragraphs fifth through seventh, under *Prior Consultation by the Student With the Committee.*)

Dr. W's overall position with regard to C's survey was that her conclusion was inadequately supported because she had failed to discuss the many technical possibilities that could contradict her finding that there is no behavioral specialization of locus coeruleus function. As he put it: "The case against any behavioral effect is not clearcut. You simply dismiss all the favoring evidence." It would be interesting to know how Dr. W reconciles this statement with his position on specialization described in the second to fifth paragraph preceding this one. (Also, see below.)

On 21 December 1977, C also went to Dr. X to get his instructions. His only response was: "Dr. W probably told you everything I would have said. There was general agreement about what was wrong with your paper."

The Student's Objective and Rationale in Preparing Her Paper

There were three factors that, together, gave C's first paper a form that was different from what three of her Committee expected. These factors were: C's scientific objective in writing the survey, the size of the task, and the restriction to 20 to 40 pages imposed by three members of her Committee.

As she was collecting the experimental papers meeting the specification of her Committee, C first studied a number of review papers to develop a familiarity with each of the areas of behavioral research. Next, she decided to read carefully all of the collected experimental papers with no preconceptions as to what might emerge. To her surprise, she ended with a strong impression that, despite a tremendous amount of work by many experimenters, there was no convincing evidence for an association between the locus coeruleus brain system and any of the seven behaviors. (See Dr. W's reaction to this idea three paragraphs above.) This seemed important to her because it matched her own (published and unpublished) research experience.

C decided to build her survey around this idea. But the question was: How? She wanted to see how much of a case she could make for a universal negative proposition. The basic problem confronting her was that an empirical negative generalization cannot be proved by logic but only by denumeration. It would not be enough to examine critically and to argue in depth about any segment of the evidence. *All* of the evidence would have to be evaluated. To have tried to present this critical evaluation in her paper would have taken several times as much space as she had been allowed and would have been futile in any case because the reader could not safely accept her judgment without going back to the original research papers.

Instead, C decided on an innovative approach. She evaluated each paper critically for its evidential value in relation to her thesis. But rather than argue her evaluation explicitly, she presented for each paper the significant conditions and findings that the knowledgeable reader would need in order to make his own evaluation. To give the reader confidence in what she was doing, she presented at length in her "Introduction" a discussion of the technical difficulties that are important in evaluating this kind of research.

C praised those few papers that she admired. On the other hand, so that her paper could be published without gaining the ill-will of important figures in the field, she minimized explicit criticism, preferring to let the facts speak for themselves—and often letting the investigator damn (or justify) himself by quoting his own words. This technique of skillfully compressing the crucial facts from an experiment into several sentences is most interestingly exhibited in the section on sleep [reference omitted in this presentation].

Thus, C left to each reader the assimilating of the crucial experimental information from each paper into the final, all-important inferential decision: Does the evidence in its totality support her negative generalization?

In her final "Discussion" C stated her empirical finding from the literature and asked whether it could be generalized. She raised and dismissed two broad counter-explanations for her finding and closed with some general arguments relating the information-processing capabilities of the anatomical structure of the locus coeruleus to its possible function—which she saw as either system-supportive or as responsive to certain unknown broad aspects of behavior. This short "Discussion" seemed especially to have angered the Committee, and deserves reading by anyone trying to understand the Committee's behavior.

C believed that hers was the correct pedagogical solution to the task she had been given, and she expected the Committee to judge her survey paper using the factors that had determined its form. Although, having been warned by Dr. Y's 6 December 1977 condemnation (see above), I was prepared on 14 December to explain to the Committee the rationale of C's approach to her subject, I was given no opportunity to do so, beyond a brief statement which fell on deaf ears as described above.

That her survey paper fulfilled the stated requirements of the Committee was conceded at the 14 December meeting as already described. The survey's merit as a scientific achievement can be judged only by evaluating two of its aspects: whether the manner of presentation of the findings of each journal paper accurately reflects the value of that particular paper as evidence for the proposition that C was investigating, and whether her final conclusion, arrived at in the face of an opposing psychological set among her Committee members, is scientifically correct. [As described below, subsequent events have established the scientific correctness of her conclusion.]

Questions Raised by the Committee's 14 December Rejection

There are a number of puzzling questions raised by the Committee's preciptous action—questions concerning both the action taken and the manner in which it was taken.

While the [first half of this] informational statement is centrally concerned with the action of C's Interdisciplinary Doctoral Committee taken on 14 December 1977, it is obvious that this can be understood only in terms of its antecedents. The scope of those antecedents is suggested by the following two questions.

Why did Dr. W not certify C as passing the Preliminary Examination soon after March 1973 when she had finished her first major experiment and had confirmed it with a statistically significant replication? Why was the formation of her Doctoral Committee delayed until July 1975?

Why did the Committee assign a Comprehensive Examination task that, while it might have been done in two months by a ten-year veteran of the field, did, in fact, take a graduate student a year to perform—and was eventually admitted by Dr. Y explicitly, and by the Committee's action implicitly, to have been too long?

These questions are so broad in their implications that they would be difficult to focus upon. Attention should perhaps be directed to more immediate questions, such as the following:

How could a paper have been so bad that its mere submission "raised serious doubts" in the minds of three Committee members as to the student's qualifications to complete the doctoral degree and yet be good enough that a fourth Committee member, specializing in the same scientific area, considered it an acceptable paper of considerable merit?

Why was it necessary to reject a paper that was well written, well organized, complete, and that admittedly fulfilled the written specification that the Committee had accepted as representing its wishes?

Why did the Committee members criticize the paper in my presence only by indirection? What is the meaning of the fact that they failed to say, explicitly, what was wrong so that their criticism might have been examined upon its merits?

How could this paper representing a year's work have been so bad that it had to be rejected as unworthy of improvement and a new paper of unspecified content had to be demanded? What was the reason for removing from consideration, this very large task already completed in accordance with a set of clearly defined instructions?

Why was it necessary to reject summarily a paper whose preparation had been open to the Committee from the beginning, and half of which ("Introduction" plus 3/7 of the body) had been approved in first draft three months earlier by the chief adviser?

Why would any paper to which a student had devoted a year of diligent effort be rejected without giving the student a chance to explain and defend it?

Why would a summary rejection of this kind be imposed without warning upon a student whose experimental work was of the highest caliber and who had successfully completed two major experiments of substantial scientific importance, one of which had already been published in our country's leading scientific journal (*Science*, 1975, *190*, 169–171)?

In the light of the total and uncompromising rejection of the paper, why would Committee members sieze upon a slight informality in the alphabetizing of the references at the end of the paper to illustrate the student's "unprofessional attitude"?

Regardless of how the Committee felt about the submitted paper, why did the Committee not carry out an oral examination of the student, either severally or in formal session? In the Biological Sciences Department, one of the two departments with which the student is associated, the oral Comprehensive Examination is the specified form. (*Graduate Programs: The Faculty of the Arts and Sciences*, 1977–79, p. 119)

In prior consultation, three members of the Committee made a decision against the student, apparently without consulting a fourth member, and certainly without consulting me. How can one explain the lack of professional courtesy shown to me as the faculty member under whose aegis the student had developed her graduate career? Why was I not informed of the decision of the other three members prior to the meeting at which the student expected to be examined?

Speculative Explanation of the Committee's 14 December Rejection

There is a nightmarish quality about the 14 December action of C's Interdisciplinary Doctoral Committee that defies easy comprehension.

Underlying some of the questions posed immediately above, there is the basic question of the true quality of C's paper when judged in the context of her objectives and the preconditions imposed by the Committee. Although I have reason to believe that her paper is a highly creditable solution to the problem she had been given, this is a question that cannot be resolved except by the judgment of experts within the field of psychobiology.

For the most part, however, the questions raised by the Committee's action would seem to have nothing to do with the quality of C's paper, but to have to do, rather, with human relations and professional perceptions.

There appears to be no possible way by which I can discover and assess the thought processes used by the three disfavoring members of the Committee in this matter. The most I can do is to set forth certain facts and certain perceptions of my own that may have explanatory relevance.

Behind a facade of politeness at the 14 December meeting of the Committee, strong resentments were apparent in the emotional tone of the proceedings. Quite possibly there were both inter-faculty and faculty-student resentments.

To some extent, these resentments may go back several years and may be extraneous to the question of C's professional competence. In other cases they may have been evoked by the paper she had submitted. Let us consider the latter possibility first.

The field of psychobiology is a subfield of neuroscience. Its practitioners attempt to relate behavior to anatomical, physiological, biochemical, and biophysical observations of the brain in the expectation of eventually achieving a scientific understanding of brain function in man. Unfortunately, nature has so far proved extremely recalcitrant, so that, despite a very large amount of sophisticated effort, we know next to nothing about how the brain processes information except in its peripheral operations. In certain respects, brain research today is more comparable to the social sciences than to the physical sciences. It has been suggested that psychobiology is still at the "preparadigm" stage as a science (Mandell & Spooner, *Science,* 1968, *162,* 1442). Consequently, many neuroscientists have become perceptibly defensive in their attitudes toward scientists from other fields. They desperately want to be known as "hard-nosed" and wish to avoid any association with areas of psychology less highly regarded for rigor than their own. As reflected in the thinking of some of its personnel, neuroscience provides an example of the theorem that "loose fields have tight boundaries." (For evidence supporting the idea of this paragraph, see below.)

In their pursuit of excellence psychobiologists have developed a conception of the right approach to the brain problem that tends to be molecular and reductionist and that aspires to be technically tight. Even more than scientists from other areas, they are concerned with "the preservation of the faith." They cannot tolerate the idea that a student going out into the world with a doctoral degree obtained from them should violate their perception of "right method."

It seems certain that these Committee members failed to comprehend what C was trying to do in her paper, even though the first paragraph of her "Introduction" contained the alerting statement: "It is my hope that new insights will emerge by means of this obvious but little used method of cross-sectioning our store of information."

Nearly all of the work going on in psychobiology today focuses on relations, or possible relations, among variously anatomically recognizable systems of the brain. What C did was to focus on *location* and not on *relation.* She picked a single, important, neuronal system, that of the locus coeruleus, and asked: If we confine our attention solely to this system, but in all other respects spread our attention as widely as possible, what do we find? To her surprise, what she found for this brain structure was nonspecialization of function at the behavioral level.

C made her decision to proceed in this way after she was first given her assignment in 1975. This decision was clearly implied by her 15 October 1976 memo to her Committee (which see), and it was stated in the first three paragraphs of her survey.

All that the Committee saw was that C had taken a year to write a long paper that, when superficially read, seemed to be nothing more than an uncritical summarizing of what various experimenters claimed to have found. In her Committee members' view she had failed to display any of the higher wisdom of their own approach to the problem.

Although she had been under Dr. W's advisership for five and one-half years and had studied the literature intensively for the past year, they were willing to assume that she was ignorant of technical considerations. Had they read her 12-page "Introduction" carefully, they might have corrected this misapprehension. They did not notice that a critical understanding was implicit in the nature of her condensation of other people's experiments. Nor did they recognize any merit in her narrowing her attention to *location* to the exclusion of *relation*.

At a pedagogical level, it might be assumed that the majority of the Committee regarded the Comprehensive Examination task it had given C as a hurdle, comparable to the doctoral research hurdle, and not simply as a tool whereby the Committee could evaluate her comprehensive understanding of her field. Were it otherwise, the Committee would have orally examined her despite any misgivings about her paper. I surmise that for these psychobiologists, the Comprehensive Examination is part of the armor by which they protect their field against "wrong-thinking" (as well as non-thinking) students.

In seeking to explain the Committee's action, it is not clear how much further one needs to go. C is a woman. She is about ten years older than the members of her Committee except myself. She is a gentle person, for whom the killing of a test animals is a painfully difficult duty.

Behind a feminine manner she has a vigorous and independent mind. Although she is weak in symbolic expression, she has a strong scientific intuition and is quick to see beyond the "word magic" that fills our lives and our scientific journals. In the jargon of today, the right hemisphere of her brain is better developed than the left.[2]

[2. More accurately, what is involved here is cognitive style. Hers was evidently imcomprehensible to her Committee. See Chapters 6 and 7 in M. S. Gazzaniga and J. E. LeDoux's study of the split brain: *The Integrated Mind*, Plenum Press, 1978. The implications of these chapters for the selection and training of professional thinkers are enormous. Their book is a scientific time bomb.]

Repeatedly in the course of her graduate career, C has been questioned by Dr. W and others as to what she (as a middle-aged woman) "expects to do" with her degree. No one has seemed willing to accept her simple statement that she wants to do scientific research and has wanted this since childhood.

C had done two major experiments of more than ordinary scientific importance. In the first (since published in *Science*) she found that electrolytic lesioning of male rats in the region of the midbrain dorsal noradrenaline bundle of axons from the locus coeruleus resulted in increased sexual activity. This was contrary to Dr. W's expectations—so much so, that, for months, despite her histological evidence, he refused to admit that she was lesioning in the correct area. Because his previous work had suggested that a *decrease* in sexual activity should result from the lesioning of that nerve bundle, Dr. W had C do her experiment four times before he would allow her Doctoral Committee to be formed.

The fact that C's experimental findings contradicted the expectation of members of her Committee (as it was later constituted) is documented in the literature. In a paper in *Brain Research* (59, 273–287), which was accepted for publication on 26 January 1973, Drs. W, X, and Y make it clear in the paragraph beginning on line 10 of page 285, on the basis of a positive correlation they had discovered between telencephalic noradrenaline depletion and sexual deficit, as well as an increasing sexual deficit as the location of their lesions approached the region where C lesioned, that they would expect destruction of the locus coeruleus dorsal noradrenaline bundle (as carried out by C) to cause a decrease in sexual activity.

Unfortunately for that speculation, the results of C's first experiment had just become available. Consequently, they felt it necessary to hedge their bet by various alternative explanations in the paragraphs beginning at midpage 285 and continuing to midpage 286. Dr. W told C at the time that he had modified this paper as a result of her laboratory findings.

From the foregoing it is perhaps understandable that in 1973 Dr. W would be tempted to ask C to repeat her first experiment, again and again, as quickly as possible. However, since each replication required 900 hours for data gathering and reduction, it is not clear how this would help the graduate student progress toward her degree.

In her second experiment (the research assigned by her Doctoral Committee in 1975) C did the same experiment but used chemical lesioning instead of electrolytic lesioning. The expectation of her Committee was that she would get the same behavioral effect. Again, however, her findings contradicted prediction. Although she proved the correctness of her technique by getting the proper depletions of catecholamines in the associated forebrain areas, she did not get the behavioral effect.

Thus, at least as late as 1975 when they made C's research assignment, the members of the Committee were looking for a relationship between a specific behavior and the locus coeruleus.

The next known fact is that they were immensely displeased when C thrust upon them this opening sentence in the "Discussion" of her rejected Comprehensive Examination paper: "For the locus coeruleus and its dorsal noradrenaline bundle no specialization of function has been found involving any of seven modes of behavior."

There is one more aspect of this problem that cannot be left unmentioned. My own field of research is parapyschology. My formal training is in physics and not psychology. When three departments of the University were combined two years ago, regroupings were required and I could not keep from my colleagues my belief that parapsychology must eventually become a part of psychobiology. The ultimate scientific understanding of extrasensory perception must be found in its mediation by the central nervous system. I have supported C's graduate study because the field of parapsychology needs a working psychobiologist who will attempt to bridge the two fields.

On 28 November 1977, two days before C submitted her Comprehensive Examination paper, I questioned Dr. Y about his failure to mention me or my parapsychology course in the minutes he had prepared of the organizational meeting of the departmental neuroscience group that I had attended on 18 November. He explained to me that parapsychology is not a part of neuroscience as he defines the field, that he does not want me to be listed as a faculty member of the newly formed neuroscience group of the Biological Sciences Department, and that he does not want my one-credit Survey of Parapsychology course listed among the neuroscience offerings of the department. It was his view that any public association between parapsychology and the work of the neuroscience group would tend to damage or weaken the image of hard-nosed science he is endeavoring to create for his work. He may be right. I sympathize with his dilemma.

C's ambiguous relationship with parapsychology through me might raise unconscious anxiety in the heart of any one of these psychobiologists, faced with the prospect that she might soon be loose in the world, propagandizing for parapsychology and bragging that she had studied in their psychobiology program.

The three Committee members most strongly involved in this action against C are valued members of the University faculty. From my study of psychology I know that all of us are at times emotion-driven and cannot be aware of much that goes on in our minds. Hence, I have no difficulty in reconciling the possibility of the behavior they exhibited toward this graduate student and the academic esteem in which these men are held by their colleagues.

Costs of the Committee's 14 December Rejection

It is difficult to assess the ramified costs of the ill-considered action of C's Interdisciplinary Doctoral Committee in summarily rejecting her Comprehensive Examination paper.

First, in my mind, comes the human costs: the emotional trauma suffered by C and her family when she learned that the product of a year's labor, which she had confidently completed and submitted, was, without prior hint or apparent reason, rejected by her Doctoral Committee in this deliberately insulting fashion and with the warning that they doubted whether she had the qualifications for a doctor of philosophy degree. Her professional life, to which she had devoted ten years, was in jeopardy. She was given no opportunity to explain what she had done or to defend herself against a vague, unspecified charge. She was told only that she could do it all over again—this time without benefit of a directive from the Committee. Had this happened to a less socially perceptive, emotionally stable, and scientifically sophisticated student, the outcome would surely have been different.

Measured in time, the losses from this faculty action have been substantial. C's career has suffered a four-month delay. This must be added to other years of delay in her graduate study that I believe are the direct responsibility of Dr. W. The time cost to me of the present incident has been six weeks spent in comprehending and documenting the incomprehensible.

The long-range damage to C's career is beyond estimation. To retain their self-respect, the four younger members of her Committee have no choice but to believe that C is incompetent. Under today's academic conditions, a graduating doctor of philosophy, lacking the enthusiastic endorsement of her research superviser, can expect no employment except as a technician.

The direct, out-of-pocket cost of this Committee action comes to an estimated $10,000. I have an anticipated deficit in my current fiscal-year budget to which C's stipends for the last six months will contribute $3000. I had hoped that, after C had passed her Comprehensive Examination in December, I could find a donor who would carry her until 30 June as an in-all-but-name Ph.D.

Because of the Committee's refusal to examine C before the end of the calendar year 1977, she was forced to withdraw (as they knew she would be) an already-submitted $7000 American Association of University Women predoctoral fellowship application for the fiscal year beginning 1 July 1978. [The fact of her pending application was given in C's 30 November 1977 transmitting memo to her Committee. The memo is omitted from this presentation.] In the coming year she had planned to write her dissertation and journal papers and to undertake additional research. Because of her special circumstances I had believed that her chances for the fellowship were excellent.

My present concern is to prevent the cost of this episode from sky-rocketting still further. If the realities of what has happened are widely exposed, there would seem to be no escape from unmitigated personal enmities that would further damage C professionally and that would jeopardize some of the congenial relationships between my departmental colleagues and myself that I had hoped would continue to the end of my career.

The foregoing report was completed by the end of January 1978 and should be considered in the light of what followed thereafter.

The Preparation and Submission of the Second Comprehensive Examination Paper

After thinking for two weeks about what kind of second paper might satisfy her Committee, C decided that, regardless of the Committee's possible displeasure, there was nothing of importance she could honestly say about the locus coeruleus in relation to behavior that did not hinge upon her conclusion from her first paper, namely, that there is no evidence of association between this neuronal system and any specific behavior. In the end, she decided to retain the form and essential message of the original paper, but to rewrite it thoroughly to meet the interests and individual expectations of her Committee members.

This time, to avoid disappointing her Committee, she submitted for criticism a xerox of her handwritten first draft to each member on about 16 February 1978 and conferred with Drs. W, Y, and Z individually on 28 February. (Dr. X was too busy to confer.) There were few significant criticisms. Dr. Y suggested re-ordering and expansion. He showed enthusiasm and raised the possibility of publication—even suggesting the name of a journal without prodding from C. The final paper was given to the Committee members on 3 April 1978, and the examination was held on 11 April 1978.

The differences between C's first and second papers are significant. The text of the first paper was 50 typewritten pages, excluding references; the second was two-thirds as long. The first paper had 168 literature references; the second had 137, of which, 58 were not in the first.

For her second "Introduction," C was able to use without revision many of the anatomical and technical passages from the first paper. At the request of the Committee members she discussed three new topics: the anatomical fine structure of the locus coeruleus, the afferent connections to this nucleus, and the theory of noradrenaline neuronal disinhibition.

For the body of her second paper, C selected two behaviors, learning and ingestion, out of the seven she had originally covered, and examined in detail the literature of these two. This time, she presented her critical evaluation of each journal article, which she had purposely omitted from her first paper.

In her final "Discussion" she first examined two concepts from behavioral psychology, "reward" and "arousal," for their possible explanatory value in relation to the locus coeruleus literature. Then she presented physiological evidence and opinions from the literature, supporting and enlarging her own opinion, which she had independently reached in her first Comprehensive Examination paper, namely, that the locus coeruleus, when viewed anatomically as an information transmitting system, makes no sense in terms of specialized behavior but must serve in some still unknown, system-supporting or regulatory role.

C found that, although these ideas had been appearing as fragmentary statements in the writings of some of the more physiologically oriented investigators for about five years, she had not picked them up previously because she was not seeking other people's theoretical speculations and had confined her earlier search to the specialized empirical literature of "specific behaviors versus direct intervention in the locus coeruleus."

The brief "Discussion" in her *first* examination paper would make stimulating reading for any scientist. In it she had given a bold, unequivocal, and correct judgment of the empirical evidence, and in addition, without knowledge of the speculations of the leaders in the field, and using only scientific common sense, she aligned herself with the currently emerging views about the locus coeruleus.

The foregoing evaluation of C's two survey papers is supported by a long review titled "The Locus Coeruleus: Neurobiology of a Central Noradrenergic Nucleus" by D. G. Amaral and H. M. Sinnamon (*Progress in Neurobiology, 9* [1977], 147–196) which arrived in our library on 24 January 1978, while C was preparing her second paper. She deferred reading it until she had completed her paper on 27 March because it was evident from the title that, in some sense, it would duplicate what she was doing. She mentioned to Drs. W, Y and Z, on or before 28 February, her awareness of this paper and her plan not to read it.

The Committee Examination on 11 April 1978

On 11 April 1978 the Committee examined C for 90 minutes. After dismissing her, the four other members of the Committee agreed that, while her second paper was a marked improvement over the first, she had failed in its defense.

After discussing at length the immorality of doing so, three of the Committee members agreed (Dr. X having already left) that, in view of the length of time C had been at the University, they would pass her but that she must be told that she would never receive a recommendation for a research position from any of them.

Because psychobiology is not a field in which I have knowledge in depth, I was unable to take a position with the Committee members as to the validity of their evaluation of C's oral performance. The best I can do now is to report her later comments and to offer some observations of my own.

In view of her previous experience with the Committee, C entered the examination at a psychological disadvantage. The Committee did not follow the customary procedure of helping the student to relax by asking her for a five-minute presentation of the nature and significance of what she had done but began immediately with the cross-examination. C said later that some of the questions were legitimate and some not, but that after the first few minutes she was in a state of panic and her principal effort was toward trying to keep the words flowing and to maintain her composure.

C believes that for several of the questions to which she gave an inadequate or confused response, she knew the correct answer fully and could have produced it, given time and no pressure. (Example: How does one measure noradrenergic turnover in the brain?)

C had been led to believe that she would be examined in depth on the more than two-dozen papers in the body of her survey. In fact, only two of these papers served as a basis for questioning (Ahlskog and Hoebel, 1973, and Ahlskog, 1974). Because of the inaccuracy of the method employed in these papers, Dr. Y questioned the fact that C had called this work "impressive" as a confirmation of her point of view. As far as I can judge, she was right because, as she explained, she did so on the basis of a differential finding that overrode the weakness of the method.

Two more papers (Eison et al., 1977, and Redmond et al., 1977) were used as a basis for a complaint by Dr. X that C had not referenced a 1977 *Science* paper by Drs. X and W.

Most of the examination was devoted to papers appearing only in C's "Introduction" or "Discussion," which she had not reviewed for many months. While no limits can properly be set upon the scope of a Comprehensive Examination, when the student has been told to survey papers on a restricted subject, one would expect the emphasis of the examination to correspond thereto.

Dr. Z's only question was approximately as follows: "You have postulated alternative hypotheses for the function of the locus coeruleus. Any hypothesis must be scientifically testable. You have nothing on that in your paper. I would like you to describe now an experiment to show that the locus coeruleus is the central nervous system analog of the peripheral sympathetic nervous system." Future experiments were not within the scope of C's review assignment, and this request for a major, off-the-cuff, creative proposal was inappropriate.

Dr. X berated C loudly and at length for "setting up a straw man" by her argument that the locus coeruleus has no regulating function for any specific behavior. "That," he said, "was known in the '60s."

This is a nice ploy in scholarly oneupmanship. After the student spends a year discovering and pinning down an important scientific generalization, tell her that everyone else has known it for ten years. The question remains: when was it known?

The commitments of the Committee members to the possible existence of behavior-specific regulation by the locus coeruleus have been reviewed above in three places. Since the matter is crucial, perhaps a little more should be said.

The Amaral and Sinnamon (1977) paper mentioned above [just before the next above subheading], which C did not see until she had completed the final draft of her second paper, says essentially the same things as she does—so much so, that it is doubtful in my mind that her paper will be publishable.[3] This is shown by the first paragraph of Amaral and Sinnamon's final discussion as follows (p. 181):

> The paradigms which have guided research on the function of the locus coeruleus require reappraisal. Seen together, the theories which postulate the locus coeruleus to be a necessary or even exclusive agent in the production of arousal, reinforcement, REM sleep, etc., seem to impose an overwhelming burden on the nucleus. These approaches underestimate the complexity of these functions and perhaps overestimate the importance of this small nucleus. The locus coeruleus may not be essential for any of these functions. Rather, its anatomical and physiological profile predicts a modulatory role.

Two points might be made in this connection: (1) These ideas are new enough that they deserved this 50-page Amaral and Sinnamon review. (2) These authors thank eleven readers of early versions of their paper, and the list reads like a *Who's Who* in brain research. If two, established scientists with this kind of assistance were needed to produce this paper, C's predoctoral, unassisted paper, reaching the same conclusion, should be admired as a tour-de-force.

[3. My doubt was unjustified. Dr. Clark's paper was so well conceived that it has since been accepted and published in *Behavioral and Neural Biology* with the editor's knowledge that it overlapped the Amaral and Sinnamon paper.]

Although the existence of the Amaral and Sinnamon paper was known to at least three out of the four other members of the Committee, it was not mentioned in the oral examination.

The postexamination discussion by the Committee included the sarcastic complaint that C had mispronounced several scientist's names. "She speaks like an outsider."

As evidence of her ignorance, it was mentioned that C could not give (under duress) the chemical name of an alpha-adrenergic blocker. This was a topic that appeared only in her final "Discussion." The question is trivial.

It was pointed out to me as an indication of C's incompetence that she did not know to where the nigra-striatal nerve bundle projects—a system with which she was not directly concerned. I checked later in M. B. Carpenter's *Core Text of Neuroanatomy*. This system is far from simple.

The Question of the Professional Competence of the Student

Ostensibly on the basis of a 90-minute examination, conducted after the student had been under unusual psychological stress for four months, C's Doctoral Committee decided that she was unworthy to receive the doctor of philosophy degree. Because C has been at the University for ten years, it is reasonable to ask whether there is other evidence concerning her professional competence— evidence to which members of the Committee did have, or might have had, access. I shall endeavor to answer this question.

Most immediately, there are the Comprehensive Examination papers that C prepared for the Committee—either of which, as far as I can judge, and for the reasons explained above, establish her as a creative scholar. The rest of the Committee thinks otherwise. [As already noted, the second of these papers has since been published.]

Drs. W, Y, and Z met with C privately several times in the last five months in connection with her Comprehensive Examination papers. Some of these meetings have been described above. C believes she performed acceptably in every case. Dr. X received all documents, but he let it be known that he was too busy to confer with her.

C has taken courses with Committee members as follows (where the grade *S* stands for "satisfactory" in a course given without the usual letter-grading scale):

Instructor	*Course name*	*Term*	*Class hrs./wk.*	*Letter grade*
W and X	Seminar in aggression and reproductive behavior	Spring 1971	3	A
Y	Neuropharmacology	Winter 1974	3	A
W	Seminar in reproductive behavior	Spring 1974	3	S

It is evident that, with the exception of Dr. Z, the members of the Committee have had earlier opportunities to assess C's intellectual ability and that, in all cases, they gave her the highest possible performance rating.

C has never had a course from me. However, she took a first term of physical chemistry in the Fall of 1969 from Dr. Frederick Kaufman with a *B* grade, and the second term in the Fall of 1970 from Dr. R. S. Craig with a grade of *A*. She had been away from calculus for 18 years and was auditing a calculus course when she received the above *B* grade. I know these chemistry professors and the kind of course they give. Because of the nature of the subject matter, success in a course in physical chemistry is an excellent indicator of a student's intellectual power. I am satisfied that C's overall grade average of 3.4 [on the scale 0–4] accurately reflects her scholastic ability.

I shall next present some information that is relevant only in so far as it precludes any possibility that the Committee's action might reflect an unmentioned personality defect in the student.

In 1967, before I agreed to accept C as a graduate student, I ascertained that in her eight years of high-school employment she was a happy, successful, no-nonsense, science teacher, loved by her students and warmly appreciated by her peers and administrators. She left a well-established career, at a cost since then of over $100,000 in income difference, plus lost pension and insurance fringe benefits. She took this step, not as an escape from teaching,

but because she has an irresistable curiosity that had been chan-
neled into science while she was a high-school student.

By all who know her, it is agreed that C is unassuming, helpful,
cheerful, considerate of the feelings of others, neat in the laboratory, conscientious in handling borrowed equipment, and a mo-
rale-builder among employees and students. She has been exceptionally cooperative with her fellow students and employees in
sharing facilities, in the care of animals, and in giving assistance
when asked. She is a well adjusted woman, neither flaunting nor
hiding her femininity. She has a daughter who recently graduated
from this University and is now happily employed in a responsible
position.

The most important single indicator of a student's promise as an
experimental scientist is overall performance on the doctoral research assignment. C's doctoral research has been described in
scientific terms [in the section titled: *Speculative Explanation of the
Committee's 14 December Rejection*]. I shall now discuss the progress of, and the circumstances surrounding, that research.

When C first approached Dr. W in early 1972, asking to work
under him, he urged her, instead, to try the Medical School. He
accepted her only when she explained that the only Medical School
brain research project available to her at that time was essentially
organismic and that she was interested in the more basic cellular
approach.

For whatever reason, Dr. W gave C a minimum of assistance
and direction in her research. She felt at the time, that he expected
her to quit and that, for her sake as well as his, he wanted it to
happen as soon as possible.

Nevertheless, she persisted, showing initiative and managerial
talent of a high order. I have observed her in the laboratory. She is
superb in her ability to assess and control ongoing operations to
achieve sufficient precision in each phase of the work.

It is easy to imagine that, when her research prospered and she
showed no sign of leaving, Dr. W's initial misgiving turned into
guilt and dislike. This is speculation, of course, but the instances of
disfavor which she reported to me at the time were real, whatever
their basis.

For example, on 17–20 June 1974, C attended the Eastern Regional Conference on Reproductive Behavior in Atlanta, Georgia.
As one would expect, Dr. W introduced his other graduate stu-

dents to important workers in the very small field of the psychobiology of sex. But he ignored C even though she was often unavoidably within his immediate presence. This was at a time in her career when she had essentially completed the work that was to appear later in *Science* and which he was discussing privately with other attendees.

On 5 November 1974, C submitted to Dr. W a complete report of her four repetitions of midbrain electrolytic lesioning, cast in the form of an article hypothetically suitable for publication in the *Journal of Comparative and Physiological Psychology*. Dr. W contributed nothing to the form and content of that report.

After C completed that report, I discovered a flaw in the statistical analysis. C had separated her rats into two groups, accordingly as their brain lesions were well or poorly placed as judged by objective but internally derived histological criteria. I worked out a method of templating the lesions from two "criterion rats" and discarding their data from the significance analyses. I had difficulty convincing Dr. W of the need for this change.

In January 1975 Dr. W received a request from *Science* to referee a paper [subsequently, *189*, 147–149] that looked at first as though it might duplicate C's finding. For this reason Dr. W wanted to publish her work at once.

By a marathon effort C completed the re-analysis of her data [that I had found necessary] and made the needed changes in the text so that she was able to submit to Dr. W on 27 January 1975 a revised version of all the essential parts of her November 1974 report.

From that material, the first draft of C's report to *Science* (*190*, 169–171) was written by Drs. W and X and, after modifications in conference with C and me, was sent to *Science* on 18 February 1975. The figure, table, and all calculations in the *Science* paper were furnished to Dr. W by C [and, indeed, her name appeared first in the paper as published]. The *Science* paper is essentially a condensation of her report to Dr. W, plus the addition of footnotes and two closing paragraphs of theoretical speculation. C's contribution can be determined from her revised formal report, dated April 1975, which is scientifically her own achievement except for statistical assistance by me.

In April 1975, with this report from C in hand, Dr. W agreed to certify her capability to undertake doctoral research so that a Doc-

toral Committee could be formed in accordance with the Graduate
School procedure for interdisciplinary students. All members of
her Committee received a copy of this report prior to their first
meeting on 15 July 1975. (Dr. Z was not a Committee member at
the time of the first meeting and received his copy prior to the
second Committee meeting held on 11 November 1975.)

[I have deleted here several pages of behavioral documentation
that are of more clinical than scientific interest.]

In her formal research proposal to her Committee for her final
experiments using chemical lesioning of the midbrain, C laid out
the plans, including treatment groups, rats per group, drug dos-
ages, testing schedule, and hypotheses under test. These were
approved without important change by the Committee at its second meeting on 11 November 1975. The work was carried out in
the following year without assistance from Dr. W. [This work has
since been published by Dr. Clark in *Brain Research, 202* (1980),
429–443.]

In Search of Understanding

There is an air of unreality about the foregoing account that cries
out for explanation. That there have been errors of judgment
somewhere is obvious. How can one fit the pieces together into an
understandable whole?

All of the members of C's Doctoral Committee are competent as
highly specialized thinkers. This tells us nothing about their emotional commitments and their personality weaknesses. These are
difficult matters to document, although they can be sensed, often
at once, in an emotion-charged group interaction.

To the members of C's Doctoral Committee, her candidacy pre-
sents many challenges, some of which have been sketched in this
document. Regardless of logic, all of these had to be resolved in
the single dimension of C's scientific competence. The result to an
outsider might seem sheer madness.

[The foregoing was written for submission to the University of
Pittsburgh on 21 April 1978. With the publication of Dr. Clark's
remaining experiments in *Brain Research* in 1980 and with the
passage of time, I have come to believe (as of 1981) that her

research will some day be regarded as a classic contribution to a major turning point in our understanding of the brain—and that fact, alone, might go along way toward explaining the behavior of her first Doctoral Committee. Her work, by its massive thoroughness and technical excellence, makes it now seem certain that the method of seeking correlations between specific gross behavior and structures of the brain has run its historical course—with very little to show by way of success.]

CODA

Four years have passed since my graduate student was denied examination on the scientific materials she had been asked to prepare, and time has seasoned the foregoing account of the surrounding circumstances. What perspective emerges?

As a first question, should this matter be publicized? In what cause should we ask others to sacrifice their peace of mind by examining this gothic tapestry? If we do not believe that the squalor of war should be glorified or that death by starvation should be concealed to preserve the contentment of those who luckily escape direct experience of such tragedies, can we be silent about the decay of academic integrity for the same reason? If improvement in man's lot is possible, it will come only through a wider knowledge of things as they are.

What motivation do we find in my student's adversaries in this case? In every segment of this tale as we tear the weft, we discover anxiety in the warp. We already knew that much of the world's unhappiness is caused by self-respecting people driven to brutish behavior by unarticulated fear. From the present case we learn that, because of their fears, scientists are not to be trusted as professional experts.

There is a special application of this idea, which I shall simply state here but which I hope to establish in my next book. Hidden in scientists' many reasons for discouraging research on ESP lies fear of its possible reality. Understanding the status of parapsychology begins with the recognition of this clinical fact.

APPENDED MEMORANDUM OF 15 OCTOBER 1976

To: Drs. W, M, X, Y, Z.

From: T. Clark

Subject: Literature survey fulfilling the Comprehensive Examination re-
          quirement for the Ph.D. degree.

My dissertation will deal with the changes in male rat sexual behavior
following destruction of brain tissue in the region of the dorsal noradrenaline bundle (DNB) in the midbrain.

In compliance with the decision of my doctoral committee that for my
Comprehensive Examination I prepare a survey of the peripheral literature beyond that which relates to my dissertation research but suitable for
incorporation as an introduction to the dissertation, I have selected for
review the literature that deals with:

Organismic behavioral effects of brain tissue destruction by electrolytic,
radio frequency, or chemical lesions and of electrical brain stimulation, in
the region of the DNB from its origin in the locus coeruleus up to but not
including its projections in the hippocampus, hypothalamus, and cortex,
and in tissue surrounding the DNB in the midbrain region dorsal to the
ventral tegmental area, in adults of both sexes of all species of mammals.
The primary emphasis will be on papers concerned with behavioral effects
of noradrenaline (NA) manipulations in these regions. For example, my
survey will include that literature dealing with NA change as it affects
sleep but not with studies reporting only serotonin manipulations and
altered sleep behavior. Also, I shall include those studies investigating
changes in feeding, drinking, aggression, locomotion, learning, etc., that
occur because of manipulations in ascending and descending midbrain
NA systems other then the ventral NA bundle, medial forebrain bundle,
and hypothalamic nuclei.

This survey will be broader in scope than my dissertation topic in that it
is not limited to male rat sexual behavior but will cut across all species of
mammals of both sexes and across behaviors other than sex.

On the other hand, my dissertation will be broader than this survey by
including the literature that deals with physical and chemical brain manipulations outside the midbrain that have resulted in changed sexual
behavior in male mammals, with emphasis on those papers that concern
increased activity. This will include the literature dealing with serotonin
depletion, amygdaloid lesions, copulation-bound electrical stimulation,
and catecholamine manipulations by drugs, as well as any other papers
not covered in the survey that report sexual activity above the normal
level (but not those dealing with restoration of sexual activity to normal
levels following treatments such as castration.)

7

PARAPSYCHOLOGY
THE WILD CARD IN A STACKED DECK:
A LOOK AT THE NEAR FUTURE OF MANKIND

R. A. McCONNELL

FOREWORD

This paper was prepared for delivery in shortened form as an invited lecture at the August, 1982, combined celebration at Cambridge University of the one-hundredth anniversary of the Society for Psychical Research and the twenty-fifth anniversary of the Parapsychological Association.

In this paper I attempt an informal synthesis of a range of topics, each one of which is complex and controversial, and all of which, taken together, will largely determine the course of history. For brevity, I use examples coupled to generalizations and I ignore ecological problems, such as species extinction and ocean pollution, whose effects will not be seriously felt before 2000 A.D. What I offer is not authoritative opinion but an invitation to the reader to ask questions and to think for himself.*

INTRODUCTION

It is well known to my fellow parapsychologists that I am without discernible psychic ability. When I enter the laboratory front door, psi phenomena† hustle out the back. Occasionally, I have caught them peering curiously at me through a window when they thought I was not watching, but I must say that ours has not been a very satisfying relationship for a physicist trained in engineering electronics.

Hence, although I speak to you today as one who is fully convinced—by his own experiments and by the observations of others—that psi phenomena do occur, I want to assure you that the predictions I shall offer do not depend upon psychic precognition but upon logical inference.

One can measure the courage of a futurist by the length of his reach. I shall talk about this decade and the next, which will carry

---

*As a compact introduction to the physical constraints upon our future, I suggest W.J. Davis *The Seventh Year: Industrial Civilization in Transition.* (W.W. Norton, 1979)

†Extrasensory perception and psychokinesis.

117

us to the end of the twentieth century. I believe that what occurs in these few years will be as momentous as all that has happened in the 400 years since Queen Elizabeth the First. So steep is the curve of history that, if parapsychology is not dominant by the year 2000, it may disappear forever as a science. These are two of many surprising conclusions that I reached while preparing this lecture.

I shall begin by reviewing some of the certainties of the next 18 years, with which most of you, I am sure, are already familiar.

ENERGY PRINCIPLES

Energy is not the only determinant of man's future, but it is pivotal, as I shall briefly explain. Energy is the capacity for doing work. Controlled energy moves ourselves and our cars; heats and lights our homes; digs and processes ores; creates steel, aluminum, plastics, and glass; runs our factories; makes the fertilizer for our fields; and plants and harvests our crops. Energy, flowing freely in nature, determines our climate and supports plant and animal life.

Energetic systems obey the inexorable laws of thermodynamics. Hence, an understanding of physical science is essential for knowing what in the future is inevitable and what might be avoided. In the final analysis, it is these laws upon which most of my predictions are based and that give those predictions their measure of certainty. The first law of thermodynamics says that energy and mass can be stored and transformed but not created. The second says that there is a natural tendency toward chaos, so that order in one place can be achieved only at the expense of disorder somewhere else.

There are three ultimate sources of energy on the earth: geothermal, nuclear, and solar. Controlled leakage of heat from the earth's core will supply less than one percent of expected energy needs in the year 2000 and, hence, for many purposes, can be ignored. Nuclear energy, recently liberated by man, offers special problems and special opportunities, some of which I shall mention later. In the past, and for the future, the sun has been, and will remain, our principal source of energy.

Of solar energy currently incident upon the earth:[1]

30% is reflected back to space.

47% is absorbed and appears only as heat.

----

1. (Notes start on page 141).

23% maintains the water evaporation cycle.

2/10 of one percent moves the wind and the waves.

A mere 2/100 of one percent goes into photosynthesis, which created fossil fuels and makes possible most plant and animal life.

ENERGY RESOURCES

Where do the industrialized countries of the world get their energy? About 92% comes from the fossil fuels: coal, gas, and oil. Only 5% comes from renewable sources: water, wind, and wood. About 3% comes from nuclear fission.

One thing is certain. We cannot continue indefinitely to use fossil fuels at our present rate. This is shown in Figure 1, which portrays the rate of fossil fuel production, worldwide, throughout the history of man. Each mark on the x-axis is one thousand years. At a glance it can be seen that we are living in a very special age that can neither continue nor repeat. We are near the beginning of a rise in fossil energy production that started 250 years ago and that could reach its peak in another 150. This curve assumes that we shall shift emphasis from oil and gas to coal without restriction within the next 50 years. For reasons to be mentioned later, I do not think that will happen. Instead, the production of fossil fuels may peak early in the next century.

To understand the nature of the energy situation, we should look closely at the curve of Figure 1, which has the typical shape for the production of any nonrenewable resource. At its beginning, such a

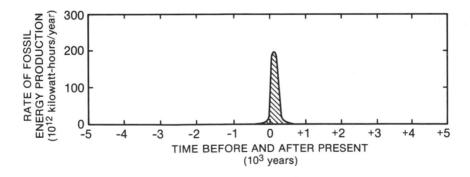

Figure 1. Fossil fuel production throughout history. (M. King Hubbert. *U.S. Energy Resources: A Review as of 1972.*)

curve rises more or less exponentially because of positive feedback. Eventually, any exhaustible resource becomes scarce, the cost of production increases, and the amount of production peaks and then falls away. As it melts toward zero, the production curve for a nonrenewable resource may become negatively exponential. Regardless of its exact shape, the area under the curve represents the total recoverable resource, whether it be oil, coal, or copper.

If we want to predict the future production of any important raw material taken from the earth, the first thing we might ask to know is the year of peak production. Is it still ahead, or have we passed it? The second thing to know is how fast the curve is rising or falling.

In the last 20 years geologists have developed approximate ideas about the production curves for many natural resources. Consider fossil fuel production as shown in Table 1. Oil production in the 48 United States reached its peak about 1970.[2] Worldwide, oil production will peak about 1995. The largest fraction of the world's energy still comes from oil. It is evident that this fuel will be desperately short from now on.

Gas is an ideal fuel for almost every purpose but moving vehicles. At our present rate of consumption, there seems to be enough of it to carry us into the next century.

For the longer run, there is coal, together with oil shale and tar sands. Unfortunately, the extraction of these solid fossil fuels creates wastelands and uses vast quantities of fresh water, which is in short supply. In addition, it is now evident that the burning of hydrocarbon fuel is increasing the carbon dioxide in the earth's atmosphere by a measurable amount each year. I shall discuss that later.

What are the prospects for nuclear fission, for which there are still abundant uranium reserves? The physical barriers to the further development of fission power would seem to be capital and operating costs and difficulties in handling and storing radioactive materials. Most technically sophisticated scientists now agree that nuclear fission is a scientific success but an engineering nightmare and that it must be abandoned as quickly as possible. Even the bravest now doubt that the Devil can deliver on His half of our Faustian bargain.

Nuclear fusion and nuclear fission have quite different prospects. Fusion is, in fact, the only long-range hope we have for a future, energy-rich civilization, but it is not yet known whether it will be technically and economically feasible. In any case, fusion cannot

Table 1
FOSSIL FUEL PRODUCTION
(Speculative)

	U.S.A.		Remainder of Industrial World	
	Peak Year	Fraction of Total Energy (1970)	Peak Year	Fraction of Total Energy (1970)
Oil	1970	44%	1995	62%
Gas	1990	33%	2015	5%
Coal	2050	18%	2100	28%

make an important contribution to world energy consumption until well into the twenty-first century. It will be of no help in the next 18 years.

The two most promising energy sources today are conservation and the rays from the sun. Together with fusion (if it becomes practicable), these sources might form a satisfactory basis for a technological civilization reaching into the indefinite future.

If the long-range energy prospect is not hopeless, you might be tempted erroneously to assume that energy problems will not be very important in the next 18 years. Social tensions are created by the difference between expectations and realizations. Expectations arise based on past experiences and upon observation of what others have achieved. A forced shifting to new energy sources and the resulting general but unequal decline in standard of living can be expected to result in great differences between the expectations and realizations in large segments of society and to cause, in turn, profound and ubiquitous social unrest.

FOOD PRODUCTION

As shown in Table 2, the only grain exporting countries of any consequence are the United States, Canada, Australia, and New Zealand. Before World War II, all main areas of the world except western Europe were self-sufficient in food. Today, largely because of population growth, over 100 countries depend upon North American grain. Judging from the trend shown between 1970 and 1980, what will the situation be ten years from now?

To answer that question, let us ask another. How do Canada and

Table 2
ANNUAL WORLD EXPORTS (+) AND IMPORTS (−)
OF GRAIN IN MILLIONS OF METRIC TONS.
(L.R. Brown, *Science, 214,* 998 [27 November 1981)

	1934 to 1938	1970	1980
North America	+5	+56	+131
Latin America	+9	+4	−10
Western Europe	−24	−30	−16
Eastern Europe and USSR	+5	0	−46
Africa	+1	−5	−15
Asia	+2	−37	−63
Australia and New Zealand	+3	+12	+19

the United States produce so much grain? The answer lies in their possession of four major advantages:

1. Great areas of flat land with fertile soil, matched nowhere else on earth.

2. A long growing season with adequate precipitation. That is what the Soviet Union does not have.

3. Farm machinery and the ability to maintain it.

4. Fertilizer and gasoline.

The last two items depend upon energy. Before 1910, farms were without electricity and gasoline. Consequently, fuel and fertilizer energy input was close to zero. Today, in the United States, it takes 10 calories of outside energy to produce one food calorie.[3] That 9-calorie subsidy has been coming from fossil fuels, which will be more expensive in the future.

This situation can be summed up in one sentence. We have come to the end of the agricultural revolution. Those who look to a second "Green Revolution" for salvation are almost certain to be disappointed. All of the grain hybrids so far developed require energy-intensive cultivation.[4]

LAND FOR FOOD

Energy cost will not be the only factor limiting future food production. Over the last 20 years, worldwide, the net land under cultivation has been increasing at an average rate of one-half of one percent a year. Now that cheap energy for clearing land and for irrigation is gone, the rate of increase is dropping fast. There is much unused land, but most of it is poor for farming.[5]

Up to now, 10% of all arable land in the U.S.A. has been lost by urbanization. In Florida, which produces half of the world's grapefruit and one-quarter of the world's oranges, all prime farmland will be devoted to other purposes by the year 2000 if present trends continue.[6]

Meanwhile, arable land over most of the U.S.A. is being degraded by overuse, by salinization and waterlogging from irrigation, by wind and water erosion, by chemical fertilization, and by strip mining. It has been estimated that one-third of the top soil of U.S. croplands has been lost by erosion.[7]

In croplands the world over, the depth of topsoil is usually less than 25 centimeters to start with. New topsoil forms by natural processes at a rate of perhaps 1.5 tons per year per acre. Acceptable rates of erosion range from 1 to 5 tons per acre per year. In a 14-year Missouri experiment, land planted sequentially to corn, wheat, and clover lost an average of 3 tons per acre per year through erosion; while for comparable land, planted continuously in corn, the loss to erosion was 20 tons per acre per year.[8]

Crop rotation is no longer practiced on most large farms in the United States. In southern Iowa, for example, the cost of reducing topsoil loss to acceptable levels was found to be three times the short-term benefit of ignoring erosion. Farmers, acting individually, cannot afford to save their land.[9]

In nonindustrialized countries, as the population density rises, land is degraded by various mechanisms that generally proceed by positive feedback to total desolation. If present trends continue, by the year 2000 "desertification" by over-grazing will have claimed additional pastureland equivalent to a square 3000 kilometers on a side.[10]

For reasons such as these it seems certain that the land available for growing food will increase only a little by the year 2000 and that its average productivity will have decreased.

WATER

Much has been printed about the worldwide depletion and contamination of fresh water supplies. I shall confine my illustrational comment to the U.S.A.

Underground water stored in past geological ages currently supplies 50% of U.S. drinking water and 20% of all fresh water needs.

In west Texas the latter figure rises to 75%. As a result of ground water withdrawal in excess of its natural replacement rate, many areas of the United States are suffering from salt water intrusion, surface subsidence, or simply a disappearing water table. In some areas of California where ten years ago water was available at 20 feet, it must now be pumped from 1800 feet.[11]

In 32 counties of the west Texas High Plains where 6 million acres are watered from 70,000 wells, it is projected that irrigation will largely cease by 1995 owing to increasing energy costs and falling water levels. Thereafter, the land will be useful only for dryland farming.[12]

Contamination of both underground and surface water is a problem of growing severity. The dumping of industrial wastes into rivers and lakes in the United States has affected wildlife and in some cases rendered surface water unfit for human consumption. The chief poisonous chemicals have been mercury, insecticides, and chlorinated hydrocarbons. Phosphorus from fertilizer runoff and sewage, including detergents, is destroying lakes by eutrophication.[13]

Ignitable, corrosive, reactive, or toxic liquid wastes are produced in the U.S.A. at the rate of 35 to 50 million metric tons per year. For the most part, this waste is injected into abandoned wells or stored above ground. In either case, in time, much of it enters the underlying aquifers. There are 25,700 industrial liquid-waste impoundment sites in the United States, of which an estimated 50% contain hazardous chemicals and 70% are without lining. Concentrated chemical wastes too hazardous to be disposed of by leaking into streams, by injection into wells, or by open storage, have been loaded into steel barrels and left to rust unattended on vacant land. In one site in Kentucky 100,000 drums were found to have been dumped in a 17-acre field by one waste-disposal company.[14]

Because of industrial wastes, most of the states east of the Mississippi River and some to the west have major problems with ground water contamination. On Long Island, New York, dangerous levels of organic chemicals forced the closing of 36 wells supplying two million people. In San Gabriel Valley, California, it was necessary to close 39 wells supplying domestic water to 400,000 people. The extent of the water contamination problem is unknown and discovery is often only by accident, because some of the most dangerous chemicals are tasteless even at admittedly toxic levels.[15]

These excerpts from the fresh-water conservation literature suggest that before the year 2000, because of overuse and contamination, water for agricultural, industrial, and domestic purposes will become a major economic concern in large areas of the U.S.A. where heretofore it has been regarded as in unlimited supply. The rising real cost of water will contribute significantly to our falling standard of living.

ACID RAIN

Industrial air pollution only ten years ago was regarded as a local problem to be solved by high smokestacks and windy weather. Now we have discovered that sulfur and nitrogen emissions from high stacks can affect areas a thousand kilometers away. Acid rain from coal burning power plants in the Ohio River valley is damaging forests and lakes in New England and Canada.[16]

The Adirondack Mountains of New York State have 217 sizeable lakes. In the 1930s the acidity of these lakes ranged in pH mostly from 6 to 9 and only 4% had a pH of less than 5. By 1975, 51% of all lakes showed a pH of less than 5, and 46% were devoid of fish.[17] In Sweden, 15,000 lakes are now fishless due to acid rain.[18]

By the year 2000, either conditions downwind from industrial areas will be much worse than they are now or methods of controlling noxious emissions from power and chemical plants will have substantially raised the cost of living.[19]

CARBON DIOXIDE

It is now certain that the carbon dioxide content of the atmosphere of the earth is increasing as a result of the burning of fossil fuels. In the last 20 years carbon dioxide in the atmosphere has risen worldwide at the rate of one-quarter of one percent per year.[20]

A substantial body of expert opinion predicts that this carbon dioxide increase will raise the earth's temperature because of a "greenhouse" effect in the upper atmosphere. A typical estimate for the rise in temperature by the end of the century is 1° Centigrade on the average, and 3° or 4° in the polar regions. Thereafter, if this warming continues, the Arctic ice pack will melt—perhaps sometime in the next century. It is believed that such melting will be irreversible because, with a decreasing albedo, more of the sun's rays will be absorbed in the Arctic areas, thus providing positive feedback for further temperature rise.[21]

If the Arctic ice pack melts, there will be major worldwide changes in temperature and rain patterns because of the loss of weather-driving power in the polar-tropical heat engine. In my own thinking, I assign a probability of 0.8 to the proposition that most of our coal reserves can never be used without precipitating a world catastrophe.

FORESTS

Forests are usually thought of as useful to man as sources of lumber and fuel, but they are even more important in their ecological function. Particularly in the tropics, where rains can be seasonal and torrential, forests slow the flow of water, thereby preventing floods and the loss of soil and providing dry-season irrigation. The cutting of forests is the first step in the destruction of the river systems that they feed.

One-fifth of the world's land surface is now covered by dense forests. Between now and 2000 A.D., industrialized countries are projected to lose only a little of their forests. Nonindustrialized countries, however, will lose 40% of what they now have as they clear the land for fuel and farming.[22]

One example of the problem can be studied in the Himalayan watershed. About 500 million people in India, Pakistan, and Bangladesh live in the alluvial valleys fed from the Himalayan highlands. The Himalayan forests control the monsoon floods and make life possible in the lower valleys. However, the mountain people are increasing in number by 2% a year. They see no choice but to cut down the forests to allow food planting and animal grazing, thereby slowly converting forest ecosystems into alpine barrens. Meanwhile, downstream, where the bulk of the people live, the effects are alternate flooding and lowering of the water table, and the silting of reservoirs. As a result, the once rich alluvial plains are losing their productivity even while their populations are continuing to grow. It is an unfolding tragedy from which no escape is foreseen.[23]

PRODIGALITY'S END

Is the future really as bleak as I have painted it? Are those of us who love technology completely out of place from now on?

Let us suppose that nuclear fusion can provide us with all the energy we need, and that we abandon carbonaceous fuels and

Table 3
U.S.A. Depletion Parameters for Some
Important Metal Ores.

(Data are by R. A. Arndt and L. D. Roper as reported in L. D. Roper: *Where Have All the Metals Gone?* Blacksburg, Virginia: University Publications, 1976.)

	Half-gone Date	Gone by 2000 A.D.
Gold	1916	95%
Lead	1958	70%
Mercury	1916	80%
Platinum	1941	90%
Silver	1938	80%
Zinc	1968	70%
Aluminum	1966–1986	60–90%
Iron	1962–2021	40–80%
Nickel	1972–2010	40–85%
Tungsten	1962–1981	65–95%

drive our vehicles with hydrogen made from water. Can we continue as an industrial civilization?

For the answer to that question let us look at the United States reserves of some of the metals that are needed for a technological way of life. At the top of Table 3, I have shown some highly depleted metal ores about which we have relatively precise knowledge. At the bottom, are moderately depleted ores for which we cannot yet make accurate predictions.

Even though United States metal ores are largely gone, severe worldwide metal shortages will not occur until the next century. The immediate importance of these impending shortages is that they signal a time of change. The price of metals is rising sharply, both because rich ores are becoming scarce and because the energy to extract them is rising in cost. As the real price of metals rises for the industrial world, our standard of living must fall.

Physically speaking, industrial civilization represents order in a chaotic world. To maintain that order, the second law of thermodynamics requires a continuous input of high-temperature energy and low-entropy raw materials. Our roads would be gone in ten years if they were not constantly repaired with asphalt, which is a byproduct of oil and coal. At present rates, the average United

States citizen consumes 20,000 times his own weight of raw materials in his lifetime—excluding food and water.[24] One hundred years ago consumption was less than one-tenth as great. We have, in the vernacular of the farmer, been living high on the hog. All too soon, we shall be down to the feet and tail.

What I have tried to convey so far are three ideas:
1. The earth's capacity to produce food will be about the same in the year 2000 as it is today. Thereafter, food production will decline through degradation of the land and a shortage of water.
2. The real costs of the material things it takes to run an industrial civilization are escalating, with no end in sight. Real costs (as opposed to paper-money costs) bear an inverse relationship to standard of living.[25]
3. What Lord Clark called the Age of Heroic Materialism will soon be over.[26] We must prepare for a future totally different from the present.

In this paper up to now, I have pictured the physical constraints under which we shall exist in the year 2000. I have said nothing yet about people—how they will live and what use they might have for parapsychology.

POPULATION

The accompanying Figure 2 shows the relative rates of population growth for the industrialized and nonindustrialized countries of the world. If these rates are sustained to the year 2000, the world's population will be one-third larger than in 1982 and will be growing at the rate of 100 million per year. Ninety percent of this projected growth will be in the poorest nations. At present, the nonindustrialized population is larger than the industrialized by 3 to 1. By 2000 A.D., this ratio will be 4 to 1.

These projections from the U.S. Census Bureau are optimistic in that they assume that food production can be increased by the use of fertilizer, mechanization, and pesticides, regardless of cost, and they neglect altogether the possibility of worldwide political disorder.

My own more pessimistic expectation is that the world population in 2000 A.D. will be less than projected by at least a half billion as the result of mass starvation and associated disease. I shall return to this question later.

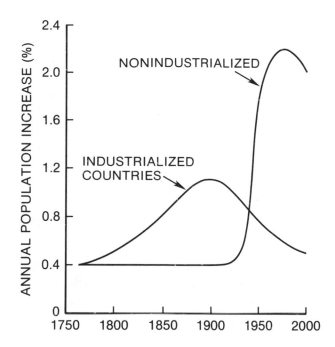

Figure 2. Trends of population growth in the industrialized and nonindustrialized countries. The rate rise in the industrialized population began with the invention of the steam engine. The rate rise of the nonindustrialized population began shortly after World War I, when the Rockefeller Foundation began its distribution of white man's medicine among primitive people. (Projections are from the U.S. Bureau of Census and assume no mass starvation.)

MONEY

A dear friend, who is a professional ecologist, expressed regret that I planned to include in this paper a discussion of financial relations between industrialized and nonindustrialized countries. "Money," he said, "is really a meaningless term when you are talking about species survival. The introduction of this highly disputable discourse on monetary policy weakens the total effect by raising issues that can only obscure the point you have made so well."

This comment challenged me to explain in a few words why I believe that consideration of international finance is essential for an understanding of the world situation. I said to him:

I am not discussing "species survival," but human survival.

Homo sapiens differs from other species by engaging in complex symbolic communication. The present crisis, whatever else it may be, is obviously economic. The "symbol" used in economic communication is money.

Money is a tool for distributing the right to consume, for rewarding productivity, for encouraging the creation or consumption of capital, and for binding the past to the future. Money is an integral element of civilization and can often be more important than military power in determining who will do what to whom.

According to textbook economic theory, the money managers in a so-called free-economy can choose between full employment or monetary inflation, or can perhaps find a politically acceptable compromise with a little of both. That may have been true when energy and raw materials were cheap. No politician today dares to say what is obvious: From now on, except for brief interludes, we shall have both high unemployment and rapid inflation regardless of the party in power. This portentous situation would exist even if we were not trying to keep some of the nonindustrialized countries financially afloat. As it is, their deepening misery will contribute to our own.

The bankruptcy of a nation, although never publicly announced, occurs, in fact, when a nation can no longer pay interest and principal as they fall due. When that happens, the debtor nation takes out a new loan to replace the old. This is called "rescheduling" the debt.

Iran, Nicaragua, Peru, Turkey, and Zaire have passed into bankruptcy in the last five years. Bolivia, Brazil, Chile, Colombia, Egypt, Mexico, the Philippines, South Korea, and Thailand (as well as several East European countries) will suffer bankruptcy before 1990.

By what magic are such countries able to borrow more money? In the past, money was often lent by one sovereign country directly to another, but that had unsavory political implications. Today, wealthy nations may make outright gifts to the World Bank and to political allies, but the bulk of the new money needed to sustain nearly bankrupt countries is coming from private banks at unrealistically low interest rates.

Why would a banker lend money to a potentially bankrupt country? The answer comes in two parts. First, bankers expect that monetary inflation will allow such countries to pay their debts in depreciated currency. It is hoped that conditions will improve enough so that by the year 2000 even the poorest countries will be able to repay what they owe if they can do it with ten-cent dollars.

Secondly, if anything goes wrong in the meantime, these banks know that their home countries will bail them out, either directly or through the International Monetary Fund. If Lockheed, Chrysler, and New York City were too big to be allowed to fail, so are Bank of America and Chase Manhattan.

The United States Federal Reserve Board has already tacitly agreed to save any large bank that is in trouble because of loans to nonindustrialized countries. Just before the Monetary Control Act of 1980 was passed, a joint committee of the U.S. Congress surreptitiously added the "obligations of . . . a foreign government or agency thereof" to the list of assets that Federal Reserve Banks may purchase from a private bank that is in danger of collapse.

In case you are wondering what motivates a banker to make bad deals with his depositor's money, the answer is not far to seek. On every promise to be repaid at a distant time in cheaper dollars, the bank takes its profit in present-day dollars.

As time goes on, it becomes increasingly clear that most of the nonindustrialized countries lack the cultural or genetic heritage needed to profit by the capital they have borrowed in attempting to industrialize themselves. In any case, they are now trapped forever behind the closed door of the Age of Cheap Energy. It is absurd to pretend that they can repay their principal indebtedness except at confiscatory discounts.

Under present policy, the debts of the nonindustrialized countries will eventually be paid by the citizens of the industrialized countries by the device of printing paper money. Meanwhile, the banks cannot lose. This arrangement can most kindly be called "collusive self-deception among bankers, economists, and politicians." Whether this is good or bad, I leave to you to decide. Its success depends upon its concealment from the voters, which is patently undemocratic and deceitful.

COMPETENCE

For many generations human knowledge has been growing quasi-exponentially, i.e., at a rate more or less proportional to existing knowledge. This fact and the availability of cheap energy have increased productivity and allowed the trade union worker to demand an ever rising material standard of living as his just due, while working ever fewer hours per week.

The one thing most certain about exponential growth is that it must end. In the last ten years the curve of human knowledge has left the exponential track. To predict the future of science and technology, it would help to know why it took man so long to learn what little he knows and why the further growth of knowledge is faltering just when it is needed most.

The answer lies in the inadequacy of the human brain. If one thousand of the greatest scientists of the past had never lived, our energy-consuming culture would not exist. Their genius made possible an industrial civilization that is too complex for the majority of our citizens to understand. Now that this civilization is in trouble, its voting members have neither the competence nor moral courage needed to guide it upward—or so it appears in 1982.

Much of the remainder of my paper will be concerned with these two qualities: competence and moral courage; for they will determine not only what happens to the curve of scientific knowledge but also how the human experiment will end.

Competence is directly a matter of the brain and its body. Moral courage is a matter of the spirit. The discouraging fact—at least in America as I see it—is that both body and soul are being degraded rather than enhanced in this time of crisis.

As a consequence of both biological and spiritual factors, I believe that, even if by some good fortune we avoid nuclear war, the curve of human knowledge will have reversed its curvature by the year 2000. Here are some falling leaves that show which way the wind is blowing.

As most of you know, admission to United States universities is heavily dependent upon "Scholastic Aptitude Tests," administered nationwide to high school seniors by the Educational Testing Service of Princeton, New Jersey. These examinations are constructed and stabilized so that they provide a standard of scholastic achievement that has been unchanged for 30 years. The scores from these tests have a mean value in the vicinity of 500 and a standard deviation of roughly 100.

It is well known that the nationwide performance on these tests has been falling since 1963. I shall focus upon the eight-year period, 1972–1980, when the average score fell 29 points to reach 424 on the verbal test and fell 18 points to become 466 on the mathematical test. I have chosen these eight years for attention because the number of students taking the tests and the average socioeconomic status of U.S. high school students changed very little in that period.

This drop in scores was investigated by a blue-ribbon panel of educators and statistical experts. Their report[27] concluded that the drop reflected a serious decrease in scholastic skills that was primarily cultural and not directly genetic in cause. They suggested a variety of possible causal mechanisms, but they were unable to assess quantitatively any of them.[28] I believe that most of the probable causes of this score decline can be subsumed under the heading "moral degradation," a term that I shall define later.

Such a drop in the quality of training of our future leaders must lead to lowered productivity in science, business, and government, and hence, contribute to a fall in our standard of living. To sharpen your thinking on this matter, you may care to reflect on the fact that in this eight-year period the number of students with verbal scores over 650 dropped 46%.

There is another downward trend in the quality of the American people that is somewhat slower but even more serious, namely, that caused by the difference in fertility between the upper and lower socioeconomic classes.

As shown by Arthur R. Jensen, 70 to 80% of the variance of the Stanford-Binet intelligence of the Caucasian population of the U.S.A. is of genetic origin.[29] The heritability of intelligence in other racial groups is unknown but presumably not much different. Social-class differential fertility is important because, between physicians and manual laborers, for example, there is a spread of roughly 40 IQ points, or 2.5 standard deviations.

The capacity for abstract thinking measured by the Stanford-Binet is not the only important personality trait, but it is crucial in an industrial civilization—and it is something that can be quantified with reasonable accuracy. Although the evidence is not always easy to examine, every other important human trait—and many, such as skin color, that are unimportant—are also largely determined by our genes. To argue otherwise is to deny Mendel and Darwin.

Geneticist William Shockley, a most unjustly vilified man with a profound concern for the suffering poor, has pointed out that in the 1970 United States census, Negroid rural farm women had on the average 5.4 children, while Negroid women college graduates had 1.9 children—a ratio of nearly 3 to 1. A similar differential fertility exists between lower- and upper-class Caucasian women.

At the present time, 10 to 20% of Americans are so genetically impoverished that they are permanently unemployable in our complex civilization. This is partially concealed by the fact that, when unemployables cease looking for work, they no longer appear in employment statistics. These hopeless cases congregate largely in the cities. Welfare payments rob them of self-respect. They are growing in numbers. A similar problem exists in every industrialized country. As things are going now, long before 2000 A.D., this alienated subpopulation will tear our civilization apart.

In my opinion, current events compel the conclusion that even the leadership class of Western civilization is genetically inadequate for the task created by its geniuses. If we continue our present dysgenic policy of selective breeding of the poor, what will the outcome be?

MORALITY

How the people of the industrialized countries will behave from now until 2000 A.D. is predictable from their current behavior. I have suggested that the deterioration of high school scholastic performance in the U.S.A. indicates moral degradation. By moral degradation I mean a shift of emphasis from the reality principle to the pleasure principle. This includes shifts from temperance to profligacy, from providence to prodigality, from diligence to laziness, and from discrimination to promiscuity.

The signs of moral decay are everywhere in American society: in the brutalization of mass entertainment, in the growth of the narcotic trade, in the increase in violent crime, and—worst of all—in the dereliction of duty within the professions.

Only heinous and bizarre crimes are still reported in big-city newspapers. If you live, as I do, in a middle-class neighborhood in a relatively low-crime city, you can estimate what is happening by extrapolating from the street holdups, purse snatchings, car thefts, and house break-ins that have occurred within shouting distance of your own home over the past year. No one walks alone at night. If you do not have a gun in your house, you are grateful that most of your neighbors do.

It was not like this 50 years ago, but I do not think that people are inherently more wicked today. Rather, they have lost their fear of the law, their self-respect, and the religious beliefs that guided their grandparents. As a civilization, we have lost our values and are in a process of dissolution.

STARVATION

The widely acclaimed *Global 2000 Report to the President*[30] appeared in 1980 as a 1200-page, 3-volume, cooperative study prepared by 13 agencies of the Executive Branch of the United States Government on the topics of population, natural resources, and environmental conditions in the year 2000. As stated on page 1 of volume 1 of that report, although world population will be larger by two and a quarter billion than it was in 1975, there will be no starvation.

I call this the miracle of the loaves and fishes. Let me explain how it is done—first the fishes. The following quotation is from page 7 of volume 1 of the *Report:*

> The Global 2000 Study food [sector] projections [2, 89] assume that the catch from traditional fisheries will increase as fast as world population; while the fisheries [sector] projections indicate that this harvest will not increase over present levels on a sustainable basis [2, 105].

Thus, by bureaucratic legerdemain, the miracle is accomplished. Let us go on to the problem of grain production.

Because it was known that the earth's arable land can increase by only 4% by the year 2000,[31] the miracle of the loaves was performed by increasing the yield per acre. Figure 3, from the *Global 2000 Report,* reveals the gimmick—which, as you can see, is a drafting tool called a straight edge.

On the y-axis, plot metric tons of grain per hectare. On the x-axis, plot time from 1960 to 2000. Up to 1977, plot the actual yields. Then lay down the straight edge and—*Voilà!*—the pen is mightier than the plowshare. The farmer will pour out more fertilizer, pesticides, water, and fuel oil, while the plant geneticist will foment another Green Revolution, back-to-back with the first.

This linear extrapolation is wholly without supporting evidence. In light of the environmental and human limitations I have just discussed, it seems likely that, instead of rising gloriously to meet the 21st century, this grain fertility curve is about to level off and perhaps dive downward.

My expectation is that there will be mass starvation in many of the nonindustrialized countries. It has already begun in sub-Saharan Africa and in Bangladesh. It is reasonable to suppose that there will be more than 500 million premature deaths by starvation before the year 2000. At least one in four of those extra mouths is not going to be fed.[32]

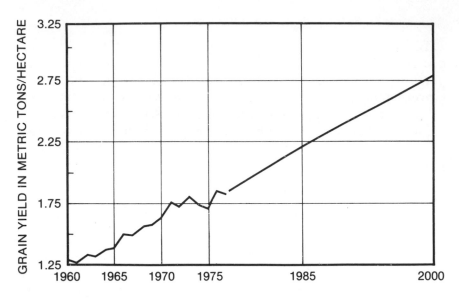

Figure 3. World grain production per hectare of land under cultivation, past and as projected to prevent mass starvation. (*Global 2000 Report,* Volume 1, Page 8.)

The prospect of the starvation of 500 million people in 18 years is hard to grasp. We cannot imagine 500 million countable objects, and most of us have never been hungry enough to imagine the details of death by starvation. What seems certain is that these deaths are unavoidable. Nothing we can do as individuals will make a difference, and, as a civilization, we do not seem to care.

I do not wish to belabor this point. I did not come to Cambridge to deliver a sermon. Lower mammals by the millions die of starvation every year on this earth. That is nature's way, and we care not a whit. Why should we feel differently about human deaths? That is a question of some interest to which I shall return later.

POLITICAL PREDICTIONS

Against this background, I offer the following predictions for the next 18 years:

Political terrorism, monetary inflation, unemployment, theft, rape, arson, murder, and riots by the poor will increasingly dominate life in Europe and the United States.

Starvation and disease will dominate life in the nonindustrialized countries that are without oil reserves.

Europe will become dependent upon natural gas from the USSR

and, as a result, will lose its political independence while providing the high technology that the Soviet Union, as a totalitarian bureaucracy, cannot produce for itself.

The Soviet Union will become internally unstable as the people of the Russian Soviet Republic are increasingly outnumbered by the other Soviet Republics. This is already a matter of prime concern to the Soviet ruling elite.

Because of its cultural heritage and the nature of its centralized political power, the international behavior of the Soviet Union will be more unpredictable than that of any other country of importance.

China, because of its isolation, can be expected to try peacefully to solve its own problems.

Small wars and the threat of total war will be constantly present.

Democracy as we know it, will disappear everywhere except in Australia, New Zealand, and possibly in some of the Scandinavian countries.

The nonindustrialized nations without oil reserves will remain as politically impotent as they are today.

When it is realized that their problems are unsolvable, starvation in the nonindustrialized countries will be ignored except as it affects the industrialized world.

Starvation will lead to mass migrations. One of the most important political problems faced by the U.S.A. will be the uncontrolled illegal immigration of aliens. Already today, in extended commercial areas of Los Angeles, San Antonio, Miami, and New York City, one hears no spoken English.

Scientists will search for a suitable chemical contraceptive for incorporation into the food given to those countries that have not controlled their numbers.

The major internal tensions in Europe and the United States will be between the "haves" and the "have-nots," i.e., between the smart and the stupid. An increasingly technological civilization will place an increasing premium upon intelligence. The economic gap between the competent and the incompetent will continue to grow despite government transfers of wealth to the genetically disadvantaged.

MILITARY PREDICTIONS

As the interdependence of the industrialized countries increases and as class struggle intensifies, the distinction between external and internal foes will become less clear. Armies will become police forces. Anarchy, rather than international war, will be most feared. It will be increasingly recognized that an industrial nation's internal troubles are always psychological, whatever else they may be.

A new military philosophy will evolve. War will be seen as psychological rather than physical conflict. After World War II, the British, French, and Dutch empires were dismantled, not by military force, but by psychological warfare waged by culturally inferior societies. Ayatollah Khomeini tried to explain this to the American people, but we are slow learners.

The object of war is not the destruction of economic wealth but the subjugation of people and the imposition of exploitative trade relations. In the coming Age of World Poverty, trade will be increasingly coercive. Imperialism, or slavery at a distance, may occasionally require the systematic eradication of those cultural elements in satellite lands that cannot be psychologically subdued. Counterforce may be needed to destroy concentrations of military power borrowed from industrialized countries by demagogues in poor countries. However, the use of military force is only indirectly related to the objective of war. Supposedly, by armed force one destroys the enemy's will to resist. Thus, military force is a physical tool to achieve a psychological purpose. By the year 2000, it will seem strangely stupid that so blunt and counterproductive a tool could have been used for so long as the primary instrument of war.

As international dependence grows, it will be recognized that, even aside from nuclear retribution, one cannot destroy one's enemies without destroying one's own economy. The leaders of the industrialized countries will become less concerned with unusable weapons of mass destruction and more interested in psychological warfare.

The distinction between psychological values and psychological weapons will gradually disappear. Psychological values will become weapons, and the use of psychological techniques as weapons will create values.

The militarily minded will believe that war between balanced powers, such as the U.S.A. and the USSR, can still be won by revolutionary technology based upon advances in pure science. To learn how the next war might end, travel to the frontier of science and gaze out with imagination into the unknown. In 1939, nuclear fission was a newly discovered laboratory curiosity. Six years later, it gave us Hiroshima.

The next frontier of science is psychobiology. The previous frontier, physics, has produced a military stalemate that will be broken either by nuclear oblivion or by psychological supremacy. Some are saying that the next war will be won by the nation that first understands the machinery of the brain.

Parapsychological Predictions

Before I discuss the possible importance of parapsychology in the year 2000, let me summarize what I predict will be the technical status of the field at that time. I shall give what I regard as reasonable extrapolations from present knowledge. These judgments represent my estimate of unfolding reality, regardless of whether I like it or not.

1. By 2000 A.D., if not sooner, we shall have what critics will generally agree are repeatable experiments in extrasensory perception and psychokinesis.

2. We shall have a useful, middle-level theory of psychokinesis and perhaps of extrasensory perception.

3. A majority of both physicists and psychologists under the age of 30 will accept extrasensory perception and psychokinesis as established natural phenomena.

Long before 2000 A.D., among professional parapsychologists it will be generally agreed that:

4. Within a favorable cultural setting, perhaps half of all children can demonstrate near-perfect scores in free-response picture-drawing ESP tests, but this ability is difficult to preserve beyond adolescence.

5. There are a few people who can levitate small objects for several seconds.

6. Psychokinetic control of some hysterical-neurotic subjects is possible from a distance by operators who have special psychic ability and who use what today are called hypnotic techniques.

7. What is now called prayer is to some degree effective—whether for good or for evil—and does not require the invocation of a supernatural entity, but is strongly dependent upon the psychic endowment of the practitioner. In other words, it may make good sense to ask a living saint to pray for you.

THE WILD CARD

What impact, if any, can the embryo science of parapsychology have upon the future of mankind? The answer is to be found, not in our present knowledge of psi phenomena, but in the needs those phenomena promise to fill. I see two broad areas in which parapsychology might change the immediate course of history: one military; the other philosophical.

Among the many conceivable military applications of parapsychology, I shall mention only one. As previously described, I believe that the concept of war is about to undergo a dramatic change, with a shift of emphasis from physical force to psychological manipulation. Attempts will surely be made—if they are not already underway—to use psychokinesis to control the minds of enemy personnel. On the basis of present knowledge, I see no reason to doubt that mind control by psychokinesis is possible in principle. Of one thing we can be sure: if psi phenomena are useful, they will be used by the military, whether or not the scientist approves.

I am not much interested in what the military sees as progress. Far more important are the possibilities for human ethical advancement. What are the philosophic implications of psi? These offer the only hope I know—and slim it is—for a continuation of the human experiment.

What parapsychology offers is not the promise of a scientific validation for the detailed beliefs of any religion but, rather, the possibility of an understanding of the nature of human consciousness. Upon such understanding we might perhaps build a code of ethics to which all could subscribe.

What does it mean that throughout history the phenomena of parapsychology have been in the province of religion? Perhaps organized religion is nothing more than the cultural expression of psi phenomena, and the truth behind religion may be waiting for discovery by science.

We live in desperate times when we know not how to prevent a half billion deaths by starvation, nor even whether those lives are worth saving. I have called parapsychology the "wild card" in our future because its potentialities are unknown. What I do know with certainty is that, as a species, Homo sapiens is doomed unless we experience a moral rebirth within the next several decades.

Old-time religion is dead. I can imagine no basis for a new religion except self-knowledge through science.

As parapsychologists we have been asking: What are the natural relationships between people? From our research we already know that those relations extend beyond the interpersonal isolation of Cartesian dualism. Yet it is upon Cartesian dualism that Western civilization was built. I think we may safely conclude that our philosophic outlook will be changed by parapsychology, and with it, our ethical standards. However, I am not about to write the textbook for a new philosophy. That is for you to do in the laboratory.[33]

NOTES

1. M. King Hubbert. *U.S. Energy Resources, a Review as of 1972*. [Part 1, as prepared for the U.S. Senate Committee on Interior and Insular Affairs. Serial No. 93–40 (92–75).] U.S. Government Printing Office, 1974. (Out of print. However, see *Science, 213*, 156, or see L.C. Ruedisili and M.W. Firebaugh. *Perspectives on Energy: Issues, Ideas, and Environmental Dilemmas*. Oxford University Press, 1975.)

2. The date, 1970, was predicted in 1956 by M. King Hubbert (*U.S. Energy Resources, a Review as of 1972*). Subsequent offshore and Alaskan drilling may shift the date of peak U.S. production to 1985.

"The first reaction of the petroleum industry to [Hubbert's] prediction was one of incredulity and dismay; the second was an attempt to prove it could not be so." (p. 68) As Hubbert wryly remarked (p. 70): "There is some basis for the surmise that [my] innocuous drawing [showing the complete cycle of crude oil production in the U.S.A.] did more to increase (on paper at least) the petroleum resources of the United States within the next five years than the combined exploratory efforts of the petroleum industry in the preceding century."

The referenced report is the saga of one man's determination to discover in advance, by graphical analysis, the true value of one of the most important statistical parameters in the evolution of the oil industry. The date of peak production in the U.S. was crucial for domestic producers because it marked the end of an era of expansion and the beginning of a time when a company the size of Gulf Oil would try to make ends meet by retailing clocks, jewelry, and other bric-a-brac through its monthly billing system. Hubbert's report can be read with profit by anyone interested in self-deception in science.

3. J.S. Steinhart and C.E. Steinhart. Energy use in the U.S. food system. *Science, 184* (19 April 1974), 307–316.

4. N. Wade. Green Revolution (II): Problems of adapting a Western technology. *Science, 186* (27 December 1974), 1186–1192.

5. United States Council on Environmental Quality and the Department of State. *The Global 2000 Report to the President, 2*, 97. U.S. Government Printing Office (1980).

6. M.R. Cutler. The peril of vanishing farmlands. (A guest article by an Assistant Secretary of the U.S. Department of Agriculture.) *New York Times,* 1 July 1980, p. A19.

7. D. Pimentel, E.C. Terhune, R. Dyson-Hudson, S. Rochereau, R. Samis, E.A. Smith, D. Denman, D. Reifschneider, & M. Shepard. Land degradation: Effects on food and energy resources. *Science, 194,* (8 October 1976), 149–155.

8. United States National Agricultural Lands Study. *Interim Report No. 4: Soil Degradation: Effects on Agricultural Productivity.* p. 17 (1980 ed.). U.S. Government Printing Office. Stock No. 041–011–000726.

9. P. Rosenberry, R. Knutson, & L. Harmon. Predicting the effects of soil depletion from erosion. *Journal of Soil and Water Conservation, 35*(3), 131–134 (1980).

10. *Global 2000 Report, 2,* 277.
   Although it has been suggested that desertification is often the result of secular weather changes rather than human misuse, the fact of its occurrence is beyond dispute. (C. Holden. *Science, 205* [28 September 1979], 1357–1360.)

11. United States General Accounting Office. *Ground Water: An Overview.* CED–77–69. Washington, D.C., 1977.
   David Sheridan (United States Council on Environmental Quality). *Desertification of the United States.* U.S. Government Printing Office (1981). Stock No. 041–011–00065–3.
   J. Walsh. What to do when the well runs dry. *Science, 210* (14 November 1980), 754–756.

12. K.B. Young & J.M. Coomer. *Effects of Natural Gas Price Increases on Texas High Plains Irrigation, 1976–2025.* U.S. Department of Agriculture Economics Research Service. Agricultural Economic Report No. 448. Washington, D.C., February 1980.

13. T.H. Maugh, II. Restoring damaged lakes. *Science, 203,* (2 February 1979), 425–427.

14. T.H. Maugh, II. Toxic waste disposal a growing problem. *Science, 204* (25 May 1979), 819–823.
   R. Jeffrey Smith. EPA sets rules on hazardous wastes. *Science, 207* (14 March 1980), 1188.

15. United States Council on Environmental Quality. *Contamination of Ground Water by Toxic Organic Chemicals.* (January 1981). U.S. Government Printing Office. Stock No. 041–011–00064–5.

16. R. Jeffrey Smith. Acid rain bills reflect regional dispute. *Science, 214* (13 November 1981), 770–771.

17. C.L. Schofield. *Acidification of Adirondack Lakes by Atmospheric Precipitation.* New York Environmental Conservation Department, Fish and Wildlife Division, 1976. (Project F–28–R04).

18. N.R. Glass, G.E. Glass, & P.J. Rennie. Effects of acid precipitation. *Environmental Science Technology, 13* (1979), 1350–1355.

19. It is not at all certain what choice will be made. When confronted with hard, simple, example facts, such as those concerning fish in Adirondack lakes,

the selectively educated mind will see those facts, not as a warning to consider the ramifications of an ecosystem thrown out of balance, but as the thumb-twiddling of impractical intellectuals—in this case, as an over concern with a certain quantity of fish. Mr. David Stockman, Director of the United States Office of Management and Budget, has general oversight of environmental regulation in President Reagan's administration. He said this: "I kept reading these stories that there are 170 lakes dead in New York that will no longer carry any fish or aquatic life. And it occurred to me to ask . . . well how much are those fish worth . . . ? And does it make sense to spend billions of dollars controlling emissions from sources in Ohio and elsewhere if you're talking about a very marginal volume of dollar value, either in recreational terms or in commercial terms." (*Science, 211* [20 March 1981], 1329.)

20. C.D. Keeling, R.B. Bacaston, A.E. Bainbridge, C.A. Ekdahl, Jr., P.R. Guenther, & L.S. Waterman. Atmospheric carbon dioxide variations at Mauna Loa Observatory, Hawaii. *Tellus, 28* (1976), 538–551.
C.D. Keeling, J.A. Adams, Jr., C.A. Ekdahl, Jr., & P.R. Guenther. Atmospheric carbon dioxide variations at the South Pole. *Tellus, 28* (1976), 552–564.

21. W.W. Kellogg. Is mankind warming the earth? *Bulletin of the Atomic Scientists, 34*(2), 10–19 (February 1978).
W.S. Broecker, T. Takahashi, H.J. Simpson, & T.H. Peng. Fate of fossil fuel carbon dioxide and the global carbon budget. *Science, 206* (26 October 1979), 409–418.
R.A. Kerr. Carbon budget not so out of whack. *Science, 208* (20 June 1980), 1358–1359.
United States Council on Environmental Quality. *Global Energy Futures and the Carbon Dioxide Problem.* (January 1981). U.S. Government Printing Office. Stock No. 041–011–00054–8.
G. Kukla & J. Gavin. Summer ice and carbon dioxide. *Science, 214* (30 October 1981), 497–503.

22. *Global 2000 Report, 2,* 117–135.

23. *Global 2000 Report, 2,* 319–321.

24. *Global 2000 Report, 2,* 384.

25. "Real costs" are measured somehow in terms of capital and labor and are distinguished from paper-money costs, which depend upon the use of the printing press.

26. Kenneth Clark. *Civilization: A Personal View.* British Broadcasting Corporation (1969). (A condensation of the scripts from Lord Clark's 1969 television series of the same name.)

27. Willard Wirtz (Chairman). *On Further Examination: Report of the Advisory Panel on the Scholastic Aptitude Test Score Decline.* New York: College Entrance Examination Board (1977).

28. My teacher friends disagree with this committee and say instead that the operational causes of the decline in scholastic achievement are (1) consolidation of neighborhood schools into large systems, (2) unionization of teachers, and (3) adoption of "modern" methods of instruction. These administrative mistakes have led to alienation and a breakdown in the socialization of children.

29. A.R. Jensen. *Straight Talk About Mental Tests.* New York: Free Press (1981). (A comprehensive introduction for the educated layman by the leader of his field.)

30. My paper was written largely from independent sources, and I welcomed *The Global 2000 Report* as a means to validate my conclusions. It did not quite work out that way.

Global 2000 was prepared in response to a 1977 Presidential directive to study the "probable changes in the world's population, natural resources, and environment through the end of the century."

This objective was not met. As explained in volume 1, the task was subdivided and computer models were independently prepared without linkages. I quote:

> There has been little direct interaction among the agencies' sectorial models. . . . Difficulties also arise from multiple allocation of resources. Most of the quantitative projections simply assume that resource needs in the sector they cover—needs for capital, energy, land, water, minerals—will be met. . . . Some of the Study's resource projections implicitly assume that the goods and services provided in the past by earth's land, air, and water will continue to be available in larger and larger amounts, with no maintenance problems and no increase in costs. . . . In general, the agencies assume a continuation of rapid rates of technological development and no serious social resistance to the adoption of new technologies. . . . The Study assumes that there will be no major interruptions of international trade as a result of war, disturbance of the international monetary system, or political disruption. (pp. 6–8)

Volume 1 (only 47 pages) is essential reading. In volume 2, one might start with "Appendix B: Advisory Views, A Critique of the Study" (pp. 713–721), followed by "Other Global Models" (pp. 603–681). Chapter 13 (pp. 227–449) on the environmental impact of the Study's projections was prepared post hoc, entirely by private consultants, and is a valuable source for information about environmental problems. It makes clear the futility of multi-model, no-linkage analysis.

I was briefly puzzled that, although this report offers seemingly irrefutable evidence in volume 1 and in chapter 13 of volume 2 that there will be mass starvation by the year 2000, that fact is denied (volume 1, page 1). Then I realized that if the United States Government were to publish this truth, people everywhere would be polarized into two camps, each howling for the blood of the other. As it is, the unthinkable will not be thought, and people will exercise their anxiety upon more immediate problems.

Perhaps the most regrettable feature of the *Report* is its implicit recommendation, based upon an implied assumption. The recommendation is that we should consume all we want between now and 2000 A.D. The implied assumption is that on that date God will send space ships to carry us off to a new planet. To future historians this hope may be known as "the white man's cargo cult."

31. *Global 2000 Report, 1*, 2.

32. There are dreamers who believe that a half-billion population shortfall in 2000 A.D. can be achieved, instead, by voluntary birth control among the poor countries of the world. If such an educational effort were to succeed, its effect on the reduction of starvation would be minimal, while its dysgenic effect could be calamitous. We have already learned in the advanced countries that it is the most

industrious and intelligent who voluntarily control family size. It is not likely to be different in the backward countries.

33. One reaction from a colleague who read this lecture was: "Your final section leaves me disappointed. I thought you would have some dramatic solution to it all. You could at least apologize. A paragraph at the end would do it."

My reply: "Stand aside, old timer, and let others with more courage take the helm. Just be sure you tell them all that you have learned."

INDEX